A SEASON TO REMEMBER

How Canada's Team Gave Us Our Best Summer in Twenty-Two Years

⟩ TORONTO STAR ⟨

PENGUIN

an imprint of Penguin Canada, a division of
Penguin Random House Canada Limited

First published 2015

1 2 3 4 5 6 7 8 9 10 (RRD)

Cover photograph: Steve Russell
Book design: Andrew Roberts

Manufactured in the U.S.A.

Print ISBN 978-0-14-319906-9
eBook ISBN 978-0-14-319915-1

Penguin
Random House
Canada

www.penguinrandomhouse.ca

CONTENTS

11

33

83

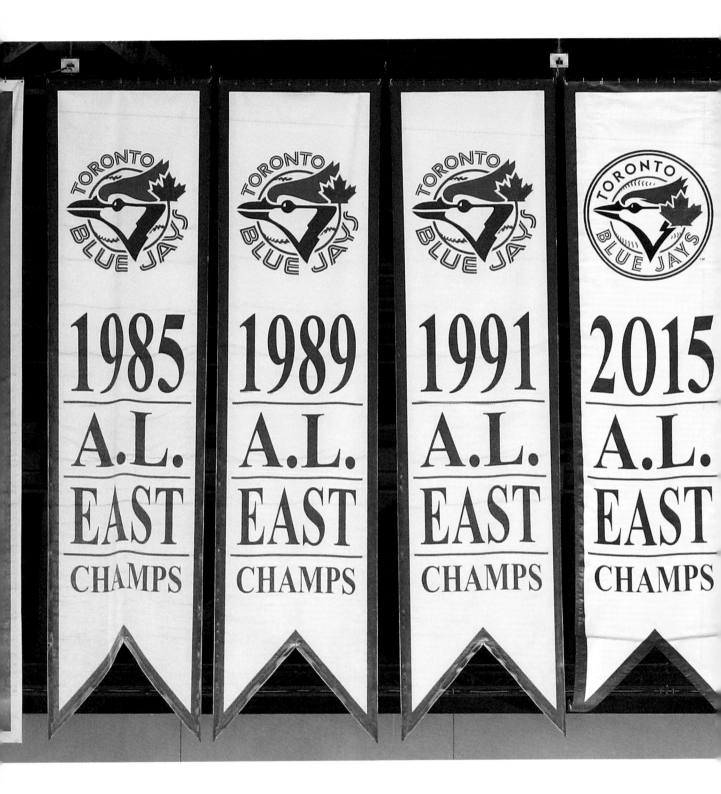

The 2015 Blue Jays joined the pantheon of Toronto baseball champions, winning the American League East title and advancing to the post-season for the first time since 1993.

BY EVERY MEASURE, 2015 was a miracle year for the Toronto Blue Jays.

In dramatic style, they went from being a baseball team with a losing record in mid season to a squad that won the hearts of Canadians across the country and came within just two wins of playing in the World Series.

This was a team of destiny, in a season filled with amazing late-inning comebacks, memorable home runs and two stunning 11-game winning streaks.

In 2015, the Toronto Blue Jays showed they were a team to be feared by opponents and loved by their fans. They won the American League East title, ending a 22-year playoff drought that was the longest in North American professional sports, and reached the American League Championship Series.

Writers and photographers from the *Toronto Star* have been with the Toronto Blue Jays all year, from spring training to the last out of the season.

The *Toronto Star* is pleased to salute the 2015 team with this book and to relive some of the magical memories of one of the greatest teams in Blue Jay history.

We hope you enjoy it.

John Cruickshank, Publisher
Toronto Star

INTRODUCTION

ROSIE DIMANNO *Toronto Star*

leven games in October.

Eleven games of heart-pounding play-off fervor.

Blue Jays games that made a city, an entire country, vibrate with unprecedented excitement and rekindled passion.

Not since 1993, when the club went all the way to a World Series championship for the second consecutive year, had baseball been so meaningful, so exhilarating, so glorious.

Different from '93, though, when the Jays were expected to win by duplicating their achievements. "We don't rebuild, we re-load," crowed Joe Carter, he of the game six walk-off home run that's been frozen in memory.

Expectations of the 2015 Jays had started high—as in the season before, and the season before that, when many among the baseball cognoscenti had picked Toronto to prevail. Those predictions had fallen flat and woefully short, while what had been sacrificed to acquire alleged destiny-changers cost Toronto dearly in prospects (see Noah Syndegaard and Travis d'Arnaud, New York Mets).

Again, promise had been overtaken by reality and the mutability of baseball as another sluggish year unfolded.

But this version of the Jays reloaded too, stunningly, at the non-waiver trade deadline, GM Alex Anthopoulos amassing marquee trinkets from across the baseball world, moves both daring and astonishing, which declared: We're in it to win it.

Incoming: Troy Tulowitzki, David Price, Ben Revere, Mark Lowe and LaTroy Hawkins.

Outgoing: A passel of unproven yet highly regarded talent.

All in, now: That was the operative premise.

Three days before the July 31 trade deadline, the Jays were 50-51—a lowly fourth place in the American League East, eight games back of the Yankees, with a desultory fan base that had been down this road-to-nowhere too many times before. Anthopoulos had pulled off some key off-season moves as he manoeuvred to correct clubhouse deficiencies, searching for that elusive alchemy of character and mettle, most especially in acquiring Russell Martin even if catching was not a pressing need, swinging a pivotal deal for Marco Estrada and somehow pick-pocketing Josh Donaldson from Oakland. Because Anthopoulos wouldn't take no for an answer.

When the regular season ended, the Jays were 93-69 and the Yankees six games behind in the rear-view mirror. En route to a mini-pennant, the imperious Toronto line-up led the majors in run-scoring with 891—167 more than the AL-topping Kansas City Royals—and free-swinging their way to No. 1 in home runs with 232. Price, the most coveted pitcher in baseball, went 9-1. The long-balling meat of the order—Jose Bautista, Edwin Encarnacion and Josh Donaldson—jacked a collective 120 homers. And Donaldson was serenaded with MVP! MVP! chants at both the Rogers Centre and all the foreign ballparks where the Jays' devotees trooped, often drowning out the local factions.

It was easier to get a ticket on the road. Toronto had 27 sellouts in 2015, including 20 of their last 21 games.

Suddenly, the Jays were *the thing* in town, and across major league baseball, as commentators and pundits turned their eyes northward, in awe of the team's swagger, its revived and revitalized place in a city's consciousness. At the Rogers Centre, through those concluding two months, the deafening roar of the crowd made it seem like the playoffs had already arrived. They lustily cheered everything, from a starting pitcher warming up in the 'pen to a strikeout to a piece of defensive brilliance from Ryan Goins to a spectacularly Spidey catch by Kevin Pillar.

We were the North, to borrow a branding phrase. And we were the centre of the baseball universe. Or at least it felt that way.

You can understand the jubilation—Jay-bilation— when Toronto nailed a post-season berth with a 10-8 victory over Tampa Bay on September 26.

"It was a magical season."

Pitcher **R.A. Dickey**

A weird twist of the schedule meant the Jays had actually secured playoff inclusion in the wee hours of that Saturday morning. Number-crunching scrutineers had done the math. The Jays were guaranteed at least the second wild card spot even before that tilt with the Rays started, so it made for a somewhat anti-climactic celebration—in theory, not inside the whooping champagne-sodden locker room. Said Bautista, "It's like if the weatherman says there's 100 percent chance of rain but it hasn't rained yet."

While not the longest championship-deprived franchise on the continent, Toronto had borne the longest post-season drought. Sports enthusiasts have had precious little to go giddy over hereabouts except for the Raptors and nothing that triggered this kind of chest-beating euphoria since the Maple Leafs 1993 playoff run.

A long-suffering, deeply yearning city tapped into that too dormant civic sports pride, unleashing decades of pent-up gusto. Not just because the Jays were winning but because of *how* they were winning—with bravado and strut, annihilating the opposition in double figure scores, if less proficiently in single-run outcomes.

In the bars, around office water coolers, on radio call-in shows, it was all Jays all the time, such that even the Leafs were consigned to a back of the sports section after-thought. The Jays, resurgent, rollicked and barrel-housed through the closing weeks, albeit not the final weekend, which had unhappy consequences in home field advantage squandered.

They rallied, in the division series clutch, from an 0-2 deficit against Texas, a brassiness embodied by Bautista's infamous over-the-shoulder bat fling at home plate as his three-run homer in game five sailed over the wall.

Ninety-eight wins over the regular season and playoffs. They never made it to 99, as the dream, the braggadocio, died on a rainy night in Kansas City.

But oh, what a thrilling ride it had been.

Here's looking at you, Toronto Blue Jays.

SPRING
TRAINING

PHIL BINGLEY for the *Toronto Star*

lex Anthopolous just wants to be alone as he drives through Dunedin, Florida, on this sunny March day. The normally buoyant Toronto Blue Jays general manager is feeling decidedly gloomy after learning that star pitcher Marcus Stroman has suffered a devastating knee injury during a routine fielding drill and is almost certainly finished for the season.

It's the second body blow suffered by the team in the early part of spring training. Michael Saunders, brought in to fill a big hole in left field, trips over a partially submerged sprinkler head in the outfield and tears up his left knee. The early prognosis is that he'll be back soon but after a few pain-filled appearances in late April and early May, he is shut down for 2015.

Two freak accidents in two weeks, two keys players gone—just like that! And the regular season is just four weeks away.

Young stars: The Jays are counting on pitchers Aaron Sanchez and Marcus Stroman, best buddies off the field, to dcliver in 2015. They will.

Anthopolous appears philosophical at first, telling reporters, "We mourn a bit and then we get back to work," but months later he tells a TV interviewer about his drive through the streets of South Florida, seeking solace in his own company.

Stroman is in tears as he calls his parents to tell them the news. A day later he tells reporters: "It's a tough one. I feel like I let my team down. I love my teammates. And with my brothers, I developed a relationship with them; you guys know that. The hardest part is going to be the fact I'm away from them . . . At the end of the day I'm the same guy. I'll have a smile on my face and try to keep everyone upbeat."

So now, after a successful off-season highlighted by the signing of free agent catcher Russell Martin and a trade with Oakland that has brought in third baseman Josh Donaldson, Anthopolous can't help but wonder why the baseball gods are being so cruel.

Suddenly a starting pitching lineup that looked set with Stroman, veteran knuckleballer R.A. Dickey, dependable lefthander Mark Buehrle, promising righthander Drew Hutchison and youngster Daniel Norris is down a key man.

Blue Jays manager John Gibbons sat down with *Toronto Star* baseball writer Brendan Kennedy on the eve of the post-season playoffs. Here he looks back over the team's most successful season in 22 years and shares some of his thoughts about what it means to be a big-league skipper.

"You try to make the best decisions on that particular day and you live with it." — Blue Jays manager **John Gibbons**

Sharing the success

"I've never been a guy who really puts too much focus on myself anyway. It's just not who I am. I like celebrating the team and everybody being included. I've always been that way. I kind of learned that growing up from my dad and in athletics in Texas in high school. You know it's not about the individual, it's about the team. We get that driven through our heads on a regular basis, so that's kind of who you are—and they're right. That's how you achieve success. So I'm probably the last on the list that I'm worried about because there's so many more people I want to see achieve that than me."

On this year's success

"There's no book on how you do it, because every team is different personality-wise, talent-wise and circumstances like that, so you've got to be flexible. But really, I don't doubt myself. Do I make the right moves every time? No way. You try to make the best decisions on that particular day and you live with it. As far as validation, that's never crossed my mind. I'm just excited to be a part of something now that's taken so long to happen around here."

Many believe Stroman is potentially the best pitcher in the group and more than one pundit concludes the Blue Jays now can't make it to the post-season playoffs.

Stroman goes for an MRI on his damaged knee and the result is conclusive: Surgery is needed and he's done until 2016. Stroman tells friends and teammates that he'll be back by September but few, if any, believe him. He has his surgery to repair the torn ligament, begins his lengthy rehab and enrolls in classes at Duke University, seeking to complete his degree in sociology. In time, he will prove the doctors wrong and graduate early from rehab.

Meanwhile back at the Bobby Mattick Training Center, the players go through their paces, stretching and running a series of drills. Gone are the days when a player showed up carrying a few extra pounds and used the spring to get into shape. These guys are fit and ready to roll.

The players banter with each other and occasionally with the snowbirds watching along the fence. The atmosphere is free and easy as everyone prepares for the long grind ahead—162 regular season games and hopefully the playoffs. It's also one of the best opportunities for the fans to grab an autograph as the players are accessible in the parking lot.

Later in the day, the action moves to Main Street in Dunedin as armchair managers argue about the Jays' potential over drinks at the Chic-a-Boom Room or try to figure out how the rotation will fit together over dinner at Kelly's.

Meanwhile back in the ballpark—in this case Grant Field—manager John Gibbons is struggling to come up with a competitive starting lineup.

The loss of Saunders leaves Jose Bautista as the only proven outfielder. Rookie Dalton Pompey, a native of Mississauga, and second year player Kevin Pillar show promise yet neither is money in the bank.

Pompey has speed but there are concerns about his ability to hit major league pitching. Pillar has potential both as a hitter and a defender but many fans recall the incident in 2014 when he was replaced by a pinch-hitter, threw a temper tantrum in the dugout and was demoted to the Jays' Buffalo farm team a day later.

There are also issues in the infield. Donaldson is an excellent fielder and his power should fit nicely with sluggers Bautista and Edwin Encarnacion. And second baseman Devon Travis, picked up in a winter trade with Detroit, looks comfortable at the plate and is catching almost everything hit in his direction.

The questions arise at the other two infield spots: Jose Reyes has been hurt often in his first two seasons with the Jays and, at age 32, is not getting to some of the groundballs that he once handled routinely. He has also shown occasional wildness throwing the ball, raising red flags about the key position in Toronto's inner defence.

At first base, the plan is to give a big share of the playing time to Justin Smoak, a journeyman who plays solid defence but has shown little in previous stops in Seattle and Texas other than occasional outbursts of home run power.

"We just need to stay healthy."

Outfielder **Jose Bautista**

Limbering up: Slugger Jose Bautista is constantly bending and stretching to stay loose. His approach will pay off.

in his pitching shoulder, completes his second throwing session in four days and says, "Felt okay last time, felt good this time. So all signs point to go."

The youth movement is led by Pompey (22) and Travis (24) and pitchers Norris (22), Aaron Sanchez (23), Miguel Castro (21) and Roberto Osuna (20). Norris seems to get stronger as the pre-season winds down, posting a 4-0 record with a 2.93 ERA. Sanchez looks ready to settle into the rotation while both Castro and Osuna are domineering in their appearances and win spots in the bullpen.

"Going in you're always optimistic, but there were a lot of question marks," Gibbons tells the *Star*'s Richard Griffin on the eve of Opening Day. "We didn't know if we were going to be able to fill them. But guys stepped up and we feel really good. Now the test, now where it counts, it gets a little bit different. But we think they can all handle it."

Bautista offers an even simpler formula: "We just need to stay healthy and everybody can play their own position and we'll have a much better defensive year."

But, hey, it's spring, the grass is green, the sun is shining and there is plenty of optimism in a clubhouse that appears to be a nice mix of savvy veterans and talented young players.

Donaldson gives an indication of things to come: "I'm going to bring energy and guys are going to be able to see that I'm very professional about how I go about my business. At the same time I'm here for the next guy, I'm not here for myself."

And some good news finally: DH Encarnacion, who has been dealing with a sore back, is cleared to play and takes some healthy swings in a simulated game on March 24.

The bullpen is also shaping up as designated closer Brett Cecil, who has been sidelined with inflammation

FAST FACTS

Six of the Blue Jays' top 10 prospects—Sanchez, Osuna, Norris, Pompey, Castro and Travis—are named to the final roster.

"I feel like I let my team down. I love my teammates."

Pitcher **Marcus Stroman** on his injured knee

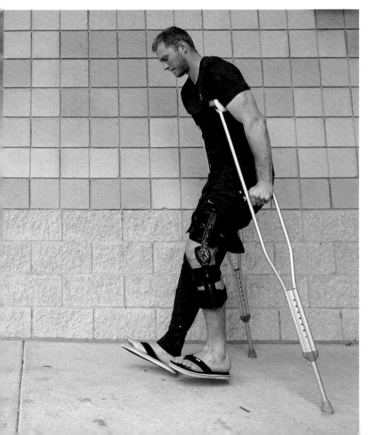

Ryan Goins   Chris Colabello   Marco Estrada

Meanwhile, three other players are flying under almost everyone's radar:

Ryan Goins, a 27-year-old middle infielder who has had a couple of chances in the previous two years to win a starting job, will open the season with the minor league Buffalo Bisons. He's a slick defender but has had trouble with big league pitching.

Outfielder **Chris Colabello** will also start the year in Buffalo after a lengthy minor league career and a couple of forgettable flings with the Minnesota Twins.

Walking wounded: Marcus Stroman with Jays executive Jay Stenhouse, left, is about to deliver the bad news on his knee. Michael Saunders' injury will turn out to be worse. Catcher Russell Martin, top, is a key addition to the team.

Pitcher **Marco Estrada** has come to Toronto in an off-season trade that sent former Blue Jay Adam Lind to Milwaukee. Estrada suffers an ankle injury in late February, misses his chance to win a spot in the starting rotation and is relegated to the bullpen.

The Blue Jays wrap up their pre-season by winning four of their last five starts and Hutchison throws three shutout innings in the final tuneup before his scheduled opening day start.

But if there is optimism in the dugout, prognosticators around the baseball world are not impressed. Most pick the Blue Jays no higher than third in their division, usually behind two of Boston, New York and Baltimore.

As it turns out, they might have been better to ask Marcus Stroman what lay ahead.

Fans and the Blue Jays players literally come together for the singing of "O Canada" at the home opener on April 13 at the Rogers Centre in Toronto.

Kevin Pillar takes over in centre field and begins a season-long clinic on how to play the position, making one spectacular play after another.

PRE-TRADE
DEADLINE

Second baseman Devon Travis is named American League rookie of the month for April after hitting .325 with 6 homers and 19 RBIs.

PHIL BINGLEY for the *Toronto Star*

To say that Yankee Stadium has been unwelcoming to the Toronto Blue Jays is a bit like saying that some rabbits have babies. In 20 games in the Bronx during the previous two seasons, the Jays have won just three times.

But now it's a clean slate and the Jays do just about everything right on April 6 as they open the season with a resounding 6-1 victory over the Yankees.

Several elements of the win foreshadow the events of the summer to come: Edwin Encarnacion cracks a two-run homer and rolls out his "parrot wing" trot, catcher Russell Martin knocks in a pair of runs and calls a stellar game, second baseman Devon Travis smacks a solo homer in his first major league game, and Kevin Pillar has two hits.

Starting pitcher Drew Hutchison allows just three hits and one run in shutting down the home team, but, sadly for him, that is not a sign of things to come, particularly on the road.

The Yankees win game two 4-3, but the Jays bounce back to take the deciding game 6-3 and just like that they're off and running. The one casualty of the series is Brett Cecil, who is removed as the closer after blowing his first save opportunity. He is replaced by 22-year-old rookie Miguel Castro.

The good times continue in Baltimore as the team takes two of three, scoring 12 runs in one win and 10 runs in another—another sign of things to come.

Buoyed by their solid start, the Jays come home to Toronto, seeking to feather their nest. Instead they lay an egg, losing 2-1 to Tampa Bay in a home opener that lacks action and imagination. And they continue to gag on home cooking, losing the series 3-1 before dropping two of three

Sharing secrets

Third baseman Josh Donaldson sits in the Blue Jays clubhouse with pitcher R.A. Dickey while he goes over video, sharing with the 40-year-old knuckleballer a little of what was going through his mind whenever he faced him over the last few years.

A few minutes later Donaldson is at Kevin Pillar's locker, gripping a bat and demonstrating in slow motion some of his swing mechanics, specifically how he loads his hands and how he adjusts the angle of his bat based on pitch location.

Infielder Steve Tolleson eventually joins the discussion, listening intently to Donaldson's advice. The impromptu tutorial is not uncommon for Donaldson, an outgoing player and ardent student of hitting who often shares tips with teammates.

"Josh is probably more vocal about his thoughts on hitting than most players," says Tolleson, who spent two seasons as Donaldson's teammate in the Oakland A's organization when both were primarily playing in Triple-A. "I like to kid him that I knew him before he was Josh Donaldson."

Donaldson is living up to his brand-name reputation, leading the team in home runs and RBIs while playing exceptional defence.

The part of his game that's less visible—though for which he may be equally regarded—is how he positively affects his teammates.

Donaldson downplays his influence. "That's what your teammates are for," he said, shrugging. "We always talk about hitting. It's not just me. We're all just trying to make sense of it all."

Donaldson declines to go into specifics about his lesson to Pillar—"What, and give up my secrets? Nah." —but he agrees that his track record and personal experience might lend more weight to his advice.

"They understand I've done a lot of research, I've spent a lot of time. I'm not saying I have all the answers, but I have a pretty good idea of what needs to be accomplished, because I've had a crappy swing at one time and I had to kind of rebuild it."

This is adapted from a story by Brendan Kennedy that first appeared in the *Toronto Star* on May 17, 2015.

Third baseman Josh Donaldson pays early dividends on the trade that sent popular former Jay Brett Lawrie to Oakland.

to the Atlanta Braves—a team that will win just 67 games while losing 95.

One bright spot in this mini-swoon is the play of third baseman Josh Donaldson, who pays early dividends on the trade that sent popular former Jay Brett Lawrie to Oakland. Donaldson, whose Twitter handle @BringerOfRain20 will soon become part of Toronto sports fans' lexicon, dispels some of the clouds at the Rogers Centre with some big hits, including a walk-off home run in the 10th inning that provides the one win over Atlanta.

With things going less than swimmingly, outfielder Jose Bautista causes more pain when he hurts his right shoulder while trying to throw out a Baltimore base-runner who has singled to right field. "I probably shouldn't have made that throw. Maybe in the situation I should have tried to weigh better the pros and cons, knowing that my arm was already hurting," he concedes.

The injury puts Joey Bats on the shelf for four games and when he returns he does so as the designated hitter. This pushes regular DH Encarnacion to first base and forces Justin Smoak to the bench. The moves weaken the defence at two positions and Bautista is less than fully fit.

Then on April 28, shortstop Jose Reyes goes on the disabled list with a cracked rib. His loss is a blow to the offence, but infield wizard Ryan Goins is recalled from Buffalo and promptly steadies the reeling defence.

Three days later, struggling rookie pitcher Daniel Norris is optioned to the minors and a day later the Jays give up on the Dalton Pompey experiment, sending the centre fielder to Buffalo where he joins Norris. Kevin Pillar takes over in centre field and begins a season-long clinic on how to play

the position, making one spectacular play after another.

Asked whether it was a mistake to open the season with six rookies on the roster, GM Alex Anthopoulos says, "We never looked at it that way. The tough part is when you have established guys with big contracts [and no options] struggling, you can make changes. But you look at this and [rookies struggling] is part of the game."

There are, however, two bright spots: Second sacker Devon Travis is named American League rookie of the month after hitting .325 with 6 homers and 19 RBIs and playing solid defence.

Outfielder Chris Colabello is recalled from Buffalo on May 5 and immediately begins to hit—and hit and hit and hit. In fact, he doesn't stop hitting all season, finishing with a .321 average, 15 homers and 55 RBIs and producing repeatedly at key moments. Toronto fans and everyone in the organization are pleased, if a little surprised.

"Every day is about embracing the moment for me," Colabello tells reporters. "You can't worry about the future or the past . . . I did that in Minnesota and it hurt me. I just feel truly fortunate to have an opportunity in the big leagues again."

FAST FACTS

Josh Donaldson receives 14,090,188 All-Star votes, the most for any player in Major League Baseball history.

Outfielder Chris Colabello is recalled from Buffalo on May 5 and immediately begins to hit—and hit and hit and hit. He stays hot for the whole season.

An injury forces pitcher Marco Estrada into the bullpen as the season opens but he eventually emerges as one of the team's top three starters.

The demotion of Norris opens the way for Marco Estrada to move from the bullpen to the starting rotation and, suddenly, three of the key pieces in the team's long-term success are in place. The evidence will be a while in coming as the Jays finish April with an 11-12 record.

May brings flowers but no improvement to the team as they lose 10 of their next 16 games and fall to last place in the division, five games out of first. The malaise continues through the rest of the month and this edition of the Blue Jays is starting to look a lot like those of seasons past, with good pitching on occasion and great hitting only sometimes.

"We're not playing bad baseball," Gibbons insists. "We're not playing sloppy, kicking balls around. We're just getting beat."

The fiery Donaldson is less charitable and prescient:

"This isn't the try league. This is the get-it-done league. Eventually they're going to find people who are going to get it done."

Rain postpones the opening game of a three-game series on June 1 in Washington, but the Blue Jays win the second game of a doubleheader against the Nationals a day later and then reel off 10 more wins in a row. The 11-game run ties a team record and suddenly happy days are here.

Well, briefly. Following the winning streak, it's back to win-some-lose-some as the Jays move towards the halfway point and the calendar flips over into July.

Beginning on Canada Day, the next five-game run is a typical one for the season so far. First the Jays smoke Boston 11-2 then lose three straight by scores of 12-6, 8-6 and 8-3. And then they slam Detroit 10-5.

Hockey icon Don Cherry throws out the first pitch on Canada Day. He also makes a successful pitch for Josh Donaldson to be an All Star.

Through it all, Donaldson continues to hit, putting up 19 homers, 61 runs and 69 RBIs for his first 81 games. And it is right about this point that Blue Jays Nation, the long-suffering fan base, comes to life—prodded by a most unlikely character.

When early results show Kansas City third baseman Mike Moustakis leading in voting for the American League All-Star team, hockey analyst Don Cherry erupts on his *Hockey Night in Canada* segment, telling viewers: "We have an injustice being done in baseball. Josh Donaldson, without a doubt, is the best third baseman in the world. The guy there in Kansas City can't carry [Donaldson's] glove. He's got four million votes. You know why? The people of Kansas City voted, voted, voted. We cannot look bad in Canada," Cherry says, urging fans to go online and vote. "We've got to get him in."

Donaldson responds with a thank-you tweet and Jays fans respond with their fingers as Donaldson ends up with 14,090,188 votes, an all-time record for any player. Bautista (his sixth appearance) joins him on the AL dream team as does Russell Martin (his fourth), although Bautista will miss the All-Star game to receive treatment on his wonky right shoulder.

And starting pitcher Aaron Sanchez continues to rehab his shoulder injury after spending most of June on the disabled list. "Everything is so far, so good," Sanchez tells *Toronto Star* baseball writer Mark Zwolinski. But his optimism will not pan out and he won't return until late July—and then as a reliever.

> ## "We cannot look bad in Canada."
> Hockey analyst **Don Cherry**

Cecil, who won back the closer's job when Castro was demoted in early May, blows his third save of the season and is promptly replaced by 20-year-old rookie Roberto Osuna. The young hurler excels in his new role and so does Cecil—he doesn't allow an earned run for the rest of the season covering 37 appearances.

Devon Travis finally returns from the disabled list and the young infielder picks up right where he left off in May, hitting with authority and playing well in the field. He joins Jose Reyes, who is healthy again and sparking the attack with his speed and timely hitting. The downside is his sporadic defence—an issue that will be addressed in the near future.

The Jays are gasping for air as they head out for the All-Star break, losing 10 of their last 14 games and settling into fourth place, 4.5 games behind the division-leading Yankees. Things will get worse before they get better—but things definitely will get better.

Drew Hutchison gets things off to a nice start after the break, shutting down Toronto nemesis Tampa in a 6-2 win. Hutchison's problem is that while he has been dominant all season at the Rogers Centre, he is a disaster on the road. The difference is dramatic—by season's end he will go 11-2 with a 2.91 ERA in 15 home starts and 2-3 with a 9.83 ERA in 13 starts on the road.

The team's inconsistent play will continue for the next 10 days as they go 4-5 in 9 games to fall 8 games behind the Yankees. But on July 28, the same day that Toronto loses 3-2 to Philadelphia, the world as they and their fans know it is turned upside down. Actually, as time will tell, right side up.

Jose Reyes gives the Blue Jays offence a big lift when he returns from a rib injury but his defence is a matter of concern.

TRADES

PHIL BINGLEY for the *Toronto Star*

The first salvo in the makeover of the 2015 Blue Jays is a rocket.

Alex Anthopoulos tells a hastily convened press conference on July 28 that Toronto has acquired five-time All-Star shortstop Troy Tulowitzki and veteran reliever LaTroy Hawkins from the Colorado Rockies.

In exchange, the Rockies get shortstop Jose Reyes and minor league pitchers Jeff Hoffman, Jesus Tinoco and Miguel Castro. Hoffman and Castro are blue-chip prospects.

The reaction, particularly in the Jays' clubhouse is, well, muted.

Blue Jays general manager Alex Anthopoulos remakes the roster, pulling off a total of six deals and bringing in seven new players.

Reliever Mark Lowe is enjoying his best season as a pro and adds depth to the Jays bullpen.

It's going to be very sad for me and my teammates because Reyes is the guy here who keeps everybody happy in the clubhouse, in the game, everywhere," Edwin Encarnacion tells reporters.

"[Reyes] was more than just a part of it," says slugger Jose Bautista, referring to the team chemistry. "He might have been the centrepiece of all of it. So hopefully him leaving doesn't affect us negatively when it comes to the chemistry and the energy here. We're all professionals, though. We can't use that as an excuse. So we've just got to figure it out, continue to play hard and look for the wins."

Meanwhile, Tulowitzki has mixed emotions about leaving the Rockies after 10 years with the team and moving to Toronto.

"I felt like I got blindsided a bit. I thought I was in the loop, in the conversation," says Tulowitzki, adding that he had been told by Colorado owner Dick Monfort that he would be kept informed on trade discussions. "So it definitely caught me by surprise. I was shocked, and it caught me off guard. I think maybe I was a little naive to think I would be so connected to the [trade] process."

But, he adds, "This is a new chapter in my career, I'm excited about being a Blue Jay, I'm excited about this city of Toronto and bringing back winning, hopefully. That really is the key for me, going to a place where I can win games."

Still, many Jays players, fans and pundits are thinking (and more than a few are saying) the same thing: "Okay, Tulo is great. But what about the pitching?"

The answer will not be long in coming. Two days later, the big bombshell drops. David Price, arguably one of the top five starting pitchers in major league baseball, is a Blue Jay. This time the reaction is anything but mixed.

"We feel we added a No. 1 starter and one of the best starters in the game right now," Anthopoulos tells another news conference. "We really haven't had a true No. 1 since Roy Halladay was here. You kind of forget what that was like. We think we're a good team and adding a guy like Price I think makes us that much stronger and will give us a chance to win. It's as simple as that.

"I did get a text from Jose Bautista with just, 'Is it true?'" Anthopoulos tells reporters. "And I said, 'Yes,' and he just wrote, 'Yes!' with about a million exclamation marks."

"Excitement at an all-time high. Get to compete and chill with one of my role models in baseball," injured starter Marcus Stroman tweets. "See you in September, my man!"

"It's getting hot up in the six!!" tweets third baseman Josh Donaldson.

"They have a good thing going right now in Toronto," Price says. "They've been in that situation before and they didn't make these types of moves. It definitely shows you that they want to win right now. You gotta respect that. You have to like it. That's what you want to be a part of."

And that's not all. Within 24 hours, Anthopoulos adds two more players to the fold. Outfielder Ben Revere comes from Philadelphia in exchange for two minor pitchers and reliever Mark Lowe is picked up from Seattle for three minor leaguers.

Revere adds solid defence, a terrific on-base percentage and speed to the mix and soon will settle in as the everyday leadoff hitter. Lowe is a 32-year-old veteran who is enjoying his best season as a pro. His addition along with 42-year-old LaTroy Hawkins gives the young bullpen some much needed experience and skill.

"He's someone that brings an element to our lineup that we don't have," Anthopoulos says, referring to Revere's

> "It's almost like being at war and running low on ammo, and the next thing you know here comes a little parachute with a crate. And it lands right next to you. And it's full of ammo. You're like, 'Yeah, baby.'"
>
> Jose Bautista

speed. "Just having that pest . . . who can put pressure on the defence, steal a base when everybody in the park knows he's going, it's just a completely new element for our offence."

The makeover continues on August 8 when Anthopoulos lands utility infielder Cliff Pennington from Arizona and wraps it up with a minor deal with the Los Angeles Dodgers that nets infielder Darwin Barney.

The additions of Pennington and Barney look particularly smart in September when Tulowitzki collides with Kevin Pillar, as both chase a pop fly, and goes down with a cracked shoulder blade.

With the dealing done, the Jays general manager can finally get some sleep. It's not hard to imagine that his dreams include visions of his team in the World Series.

Leftie David Price is arguably one of the top five starting pitchers in major league baseball. He will play a key role down the stretch.

Big deals

Clockwise from top left: Outfielder Ben Revere adds solid defence, a terrific on-base percentage and speed to the lineup and soon settles in as the everyday leadoff hitter. Demand for team logo apparel is high—in one weekend the Blue Jays sell a team record 1,400 jerseys. Infielder Cliff Pennington fills in nicely when Troy Tulowitzki goes down with a shoulder injury. LaTroy Hawkins brings skill and wisdom to the young bullpen.

STRETCH
RUN

When Troy Tulowitzki steps into the batter's box on July 29 at the Rogers Centre, the Blue Jays are bailing water.

Shortstop Troy Tulowitzki solidifies the Jays' inner defence and is regularly greeted by the fans with chants of "Tulo, Tulo, Tulo!"

"That was the best atmosphere I've ever been in."

Pitcher **David Price** after his first start in Toronto

PHIL BINGLEY for the *Toronto Star*

Yes, they have a new All-Star shortstop and a wily new pitcher—Tulowitzki and 42-year-old reliever LaTroy Hawkins were picked up in a trade a day earlier with the Colorado Rockies. But the Jays have lost more games than they have won (50 wins, 51 losses) this season and the division-leading New York Yankees are riding a speedboat that is quickly disappearing over the horizon.

Toronto's long-suffering baseball fans greet the gifted infielder warmly and applaud politely even as he strikes out in his first at-bat. Two innings later, Tulowitzki is back at home plate and this time he crushes a line drive to centre field for a two-run homer. The crowd explodes with chants of "Tulo, Tulo, Tulo!"

Tulowitzki collects two more hits, scores again and knocks in another run as the Jays beat Philadelphia 8-2. They will never look back.

A day later, superstar pitcher David Price joins the team in a trade with Detroit and a day after that, general manager Alex Anthopoulos makes separate deals to land outfielder Ben Revere and reliever Mark Lowe.

Rarely in the history of sport has a makeover made such a dramatic difference. The Blue Jays start to win and everyone on the roster steps up his game. Marco Estrada produces the latest in a series of solid starts to beat American League–leading Kansas City 5-2 and knuckle-baller R.A. Dickey, who has struggled through much of the season, turns in his third impressive start in a row to cap a 3-1 series win over the Royals.

Next up is David Price, who makes his debut August 3

against Minnesota. As he walks to the field for his stretching exercises, the crowd erupts in a standing ovation. They rise again when he strolls to the bullpen for his warm-up session, again when he walks back to the dugout, and again when he takes to the mound for the first pitch of the game. In fact, the sellout crowd is up and yelling for much of the game as Price mows down the Twins, striking out 11 in eight innings and allowing just one run in a 5-1 victory.

"That was the best atmosphere I've ever been in," Price says after the game. "I've pitched in really big games . . . but that atmosphere today, that takes the cake."

Estrada allows just two hits in a 3-1 decision over the Twins, then veteran leftie Mark Buehrle picks up his 12th win of the season to put a bow on a four-game sweep. Blue Jays hitters are feeling it, too, as Josh Donaldson (29th homer), Jose Bautista (24th) and Edwin Encarnacion (21st) all go deep during the series.

It's August 7, the Jays are on an 8-1 roll and back in the thick of things for a playoff spot. And there's even more good news: Marcus Stroman is well ahead of schedule in his rehabilitation program and there's a chance that he might be able to rejoin the team and pitch in September.

"It's still far-fetched," manager John Gibbons says. "But the fact that he's on a mound, I don't know. I think it'd be good for him and good for us. Guys love having him around . . . Fans would love it."

One individual who has quietly played a key role in the turnaround is catcher Russell Martin. It's no coincidence that the pitching staff has improved over the season as the Canadian-born receiver has learned their strengths and weaknesses. And he's an expert at "framing" pitches—catching the ball cleanly and holding it so that the umpire can see it's a strike (even if sometimes it isn't). Martin is also a big contributor to the offence, hitting 23 homers and knocking in 77 runs, many of them at critical moments.

Next up are the division-leading Yankees. While Toronto has built up some momentum, it won't mean much unless they can tame the Yanks and do it in New York.

Donaldson sets the tone in game one with a first inning smash to put the visitors up 1-0. The Yankees' Mark Texeira counters with his own homer to knot the score at 1-1. And that will be it for the home team. The Yankees will not score a single run for the rest of the series as Dickey, Price and Estrada turn the Bronx bats into fashion accessories. Bautista homers in the top of the 10th inning to give the Jays a 2-1 lead and young closer Roberto Osuna shuts the door for his ninth save of the season.

Price is dominant in game two, Justin Smoak cracks a grand slam in the top of the sixth inning to break up a 0-0 stalemate, Tulowitzski homers an inning later, and the Jays win 6-0. Donaldson and Bautista rip solo shots to put the Jays up 2-0 in the series finale; then Estrada, LaTroy Hawkins, Aaron Sanchez and Osuna blank the Yankees while allowing just three hits in nine innings.

"I'm in mid-season form, 100 percent."

Pitcher **Marcus Stroman**

Pitcher Marcus Stroman rejoins the team on September 12, starting and beating the Yankees 10-7. He then proceeds to win his three remaining starts while allowing just 5 runs in 27 innings for a sparkling 1.67 ERA.

"We pitched good, too, and they have a heckuva offence. We just got some big home runs," says Gibbons, a master of understatement.

Price, reflecting on his second strong performance as a Blue Jay, offers up his approach to pitching—one he says he learned from former Tampa teammate James Shields: "When it's not going great and if you don't like it, pitch better. It goes both ways—if you throw the ball well or not. It's something I'll live by, and it works."

It quickly becomes the mantra of the whole pitching staff.

If there is a turning point in the season, this is it. By sweeping New York, the Blue Jays suddenly are in second place just 1.5 games out of first. In 12 days they have cut the Yankees' lead by 6.5 games and when they fly home and win three straight against Oakland, they move to the top of the division. The 14-1 run, which includes their second 11-game winning streak of the season, puts them on the road to a division title and gives them the confidence to overcome a couple of speed bumps along the way.

And if the team has been transformed, so has the Blue Jays' fan base. The most obvious difference is the number of people coming to the Rogers Centre in Toronto for each game. Before the trade deadline at the end of July, there are just two sellouts (Opening Day and July 1) in 56 games. Post-deadline, there are 23 sellouts in 26 home games.

The makeup of the crowd is different, too. No longer are these the polite, reserved fans of the old days, a number of whom perhaps got their tickets from the company or a client.

These fans are young, enthusiastic, knowledgeable and involved. They're often on their feet from the first pitch of the game and still there when the final out is recorded. And they don't leave early, no matter what the score is.

And it's not just at the ballpark; TV ratings are more than double the norm for some games as fans tune in across Canada to watch the team play—and usually win. Casual conversations that once focused on the weather now often start with "How about those Blue Jays?" Or, "Do you think the Blue Jays can win it all?"

Sales of logo apparel are soaring. More than 1,400 Jays jerseys are sold in one weekend with half of the online sales coming from outside Ontario. "We're in new territory I guess is what it all boils down to," says Anthony Partipilo, the team's vice-president for marketing and merchandising.

Yogi Berra, the famous Yankees catcher who died on September 22, 2015, once said: "Love is the most important thing in the world but baseball is pretty good, too." Blue Jays fans agree—they love their team and they love baseball.

The three Canadian political leaders who hope to form a government after the October 19 election get caught up in the stretch run fever. Each comes to a home game and, in each case, the Blue Jays lose. The three politicians promise not to return.

The Jays start another run on August 16, winning 12 of their next 15 games. When the dust settles on September 2, they sit alone in first place in the East, 1.5 games ahead of the Yankees. It's a lead that will only grow as the month unfolds.

A day later, the almost unthinkable happens. Marcus Stroman takes the mound for the Class-A Lansing Lugnuts

The New York Yankees observe a moment of silence
September 23 at the Rogers Centre for former Yankee great
Yogi Berra, who died a day earlier.

Edwin Encarnacion is blazing hot for the last two months of the season. Here, he "walks the parrot" after a two-run homer against the Boston Red Sox.

on a lovely Michigan evening. The young hurler strikes out seven, walks one, and doesn't allow a hit in 4⅔ innings before he reaches his 70-pitch limit. Pat Hentgen, a former Cy Young winner and a special assistant to the Jays, is watching from the scout seats. "He looked sharp," Hentgen says. "His pitches had good finish. His breaking ball was fooling guys. He didn't disappoint."

Stroman rejoins the big team on September 12, starting and beating the Yankees 10-7. "I'm in mid-season form, 100 percent," he says. "Every single pitch is ready. My arm's ready, my knee's ready." He then proceeds to prove his point by winning his three remaining starts while allowing just 5 runs in 27 innings for a sparkling 1.67 ERA.

With the starting rotation looking sharp, the bullpen stepping up behind the strong arms of Sanchez, Cecil and Osuna, and the bats of Donaldson, Bautista and Encarnacion booming, only two questions remain: When will the Jays clinch a playoff spot and when will they win the East?

The answers are not long in coming. The playoff berth is in the bag on September 25 when the Jays win 5-3 over Tampa Bay—but only after the league's mathematicians complete their calculations in the middle of the night.

The division title is assured on September 30 as Encarnacion, Bautista and Smoak go deep and Stroman allows just one run in eight innings as the Jays crush Baltimore 15-2. The players swarm the field and a group of Blue Jays fans behind the visitors' dugout serenade general manager Anthopoulos with "Thank you, Alex," clap, clap, clap-clap-clap, "Thank you, Alex," clap, clap, clap-clap-clap.

"It's a little odd," Anthopoulos says later. "You're not a player, you certainly don't expect that. But [the fans'] support has been great. I can't say enough about that."

As he watches the division clincher, Blue Jays president Paul Beeston thinks happily about the kid he has mentored, trusted and watched blossom. "Because I know the effort he's put into it, I know the commitment he put into it, I know all the things that have happened

FAST FACTS

The Blue Jays win 43 of their last 61 games and score 891 runs for the season—127 more runs than the next best team.

The defender

There are few moments in a baseball game when Russell Martin looks more self-satisfied than when he cuts down a runner at second base to end an inning. Popped up from his crouch, his catcher's mask twisted half across his face, he looks like a marksman admiring his shot.

"I definitely feel like a badass when I throw somebody out, especially when it's a speedster," he admits. "But I also understand I do it with the help of the pitcher, too."

Martin arrived in Toronto during the off-season with a reputation as one of the best defensive catchers in the game.

"He's money," says second baseman Devon Travis of his throws to catch base runners. "It's on that same plane every time and you can almost, like, close your eyes and put the tags on most guys."

Martin's caught-stealing rate has always been slightly above league average, but since 2013 his numbers have spiked dramatically. He says he has always had a strong arm, but what he has improved in recent years is his footwork behind the plate and the accuracy of his throws, particularly to second.

A few years ago he started practising a pre-game footwork routine, which he says has helped him make quicker throws to bases. "For me, everything is about footwork and the exchange in the last year to the organization," says Beeston, who will step down at the end of the season. "And you know . . . this is his manager, this is his scouting staff, this is his development staff, this is his team. He's the future of baseball in Toronto."

The Jays wrap up the regular schedule with a 93-69 record, 6 games ahead of New York. They win 43 of their last 61 games and score 891 runs—127 more than any other team in the major leagues. It all translates to the team's first appearance in the post-season since 1993, a span of 22 years.

Josh Donaldson stakes his claim to the American League Most Valuable Player award with a fabulous season. He smacks 41 home runs and leads the league in RBIs (123), extra base hits (84), total bases (352) and game-winning RBIs (20). He is also responsible for several memorable highlights, including three walk-offs, game winning homers, a ridiculous headfirst slide to home plate to score a run on a pop fly and a spectacular diving catch into the stands.

The city and the country are abuzz with playoff baseball fever. On the eve of their first post-season game against the Texas Rangers, several Blue Jays players attend the opening game of the National Hockey League season as the Toronto Maple Leafs host—and lose—3-1 to the Montreal Canadiens.

For years, the Maple Leafs have dominated the sports scene in Canada's biggest city. But as the Blue Jays are introduced at the Air Canada Centre, the crowd's roars make it clear that there's a new number-one team in town.

from glove to hand," he says.

In the outfield before every game, Martin does two different drills. The first is a receiving drill, which he does with his bare hands.

Bullpen catcher Craig Densem will throw him balls from about 30 feet away and Martin will work on exchanging the ball from one hand to the other as quickly as possible, making quick little jab steps each time.

Then he mimics his footwork as if he was actually throwing to a base: five times for throws to second and two times each to first and third.

"It keeps me in tune," he says. "So when you get in the game it's kind of ingrained in your mind, the mechanics of it."

So how does throwing a runner out compare to doing something on offence? "It depends on the situation," Martin says. "You drive in a run and it's the winning run, it's going to feel pretty good; you throw out a runner to end the game and it's going to feel pretty good."

But he does love the feeling of shortening an inning and getting his team back into the dugout. "Any time you get somebody out or pick somebody off, pitchers appreciate it, the team appreciates it and I enjoy it."

This article is adapted from a story by Brendan Kennedy that was published in the *Toronto Star* on May 18, 2015.

Josh Donaldson plays with reckless abandon in the field and on the basepaths while making his case to be the American League's most valuable player.

AMERICAN LEAGUE
SERIES

Six days, five games, two cities and, for Blue Jays Nation, a wild ride through a gamut of emotions—despair, shock, joy, frustration, disbelief, anger and, finally, ecstasy.

Favoured by most pundits to roll over the Texas Rangers in their American League Division Series, the Jays wring every ounce of drama out of the proceedings before winning the fifth and deciding game 6-3.

"I don't mind taking on the favourite role, if that's what it is, but honestly, you go out there and play the game, and anything can happen," Josh Donaldson tells the *Toronto Star* on the eve of game one. In light of what transpires, no one will accuse the All-Star third baseman of overselling the showdown.

AL Division Series
GAME ONE

TORONTO BLUE JAYS 3   TEXAS RANGERS 5

BRUCE ARTHUR *Toronto Star*
First published on October 9, 2015

TORONTO, ONTARIO—Canada waited 22 years for this. Well, not this, exactly. There was a moment where the first Blue Jays playoff game in over two decades appeared to morph from disappointment to disaster, a grease fire that spread to the drapes. Things went wrong. Then more things. The roof was closed, for some stupid reason, but it felt like it was caving in.

"It's not the end of the world," said catcher Russell Martin, in French, after a 5-3 loss to the Texas Rangers in game one of the best-of-five American League Division Series. "I can only speak for myself, but I'm ready for [game two] already."

Before anybody hyperventilates, this wasn't fatal. It was just an awful way to play the first playoff baseball game in more than 20 years. That's all.

Jays starter David Price has trouble commanding his pitches after an 11-day layoff and gives up five earned runs in seven innings.

"I know it's there," said ace David Price, who became the first pitcher in Major-League history to lose his first six post-season starts and admitted to some healthy, natural nerves. "I know it's there. Hopefully [a win] comes in my next start. And if not, my next one, and my next one."

There's no guarantee Price will start another game for the Blue Jays and that's up to everyone else. Price just wasn't very good: he hit three batters all season and two on Thursday. He allowed home runs to the number eight and nine hitters in the Rangers lineup. He wasn't an ace. It happens.

Price faltering is one thing. Watching the probable MVP Josh Donaldson get kneed in the head trying to break up a double play, collapse to the turf for a second, grimace as he left the field, play one inning at third before being removed for what manager John Gibbons said was light-headedness: that looked like disaster.

It was a lot like Troy Tulowitzki being injured by a charging Kevin Pillar: good intentions, bad result. Pillar pointed out that had Hanser Alberto—the replacement for Rangers third baseman Adrian Beltre, who left with

Josh Donaldson breaks up a double play but takes a knee to the head from Texas infielder Rougned Odor and is eventually forced to leave the game.

back spasms—not bobbled the ball to third a little, the play at second wouldn't have been as close.

"I think if he peeks in there, and realizes that, I don't think he might have to go as hard as he did," Pillar said. "But that's the kind of guy he is, and it led to a run."

Bad luck, bad play. Then Jose Bautista wasn't in right field for the top of the ninth and it felt like the Jays were just another Toronto team.

It had been so big, so anticipated. Three hours before the game started they wheeled out the carts with the cotton candy and the popcorn, the peanuts and Cracker Jacks, into the square outside the building.

Inside, they drew the batter's boxes, groomed the infield and dusted off home plate. There were 49,834 crammed under the dome, and everyone stood for the anthems, and the AL East banner was unfurled in centre field.

"There's a lot of emotions there," Pillar said. "You look up there and you understand that's forever and you're part of that."

And then, that familiar feeling: the floor falling away, and the city's sports fans clawing at the air. It felt very Toronto. The Raptors lose at the buzzer in game seven or get swept; the Leafs were up 4-1 once upon a time. Step right up to the plate, lads. Your turn.

Except this isn't over, and is probably a long way from over. Bautista only left because of a mild cramp in his left hamstring; he is expected to play game two. Price wasn't an ace but Marcus Stroman will start game two, and, as Pillar says, "Stroman's a big-time pitcher. He's an ace on most teams." He's better than Cole Hamels, it says here.

"It's not the end of the world."

Jays catcher **Russell Martin**

FAST FACTS

David Price hits the Rangers' Rougned Odor twice in game one after hitting just three batters all season.

Pillar lends a hand

Darryl Stawychny had picked October 8, the opening day of the Jays–Rangers series, to propose to Katie Bookman.

A day earlier he was having breakfast at a spot near the Rogers Centre when his favourite player, Kevin Pillar, just happened to be there. "I went up and asked him, 'Hey, do you mind if you just hold this sign for me?'" Darryl said.

Soon Stawychny had a photo of him and Pillar holding a placemat bearing the hastily scrawled message, "Katie, will you marry this guy?" with an arrow pointing to Stawychny. A day and a quick picture-framing later, there he was in the middle of Blue Jays Way, dropped on one knee before the game.

"All of a sudden he stopped. He opens his backpack and pulls out this frame, and Kevin Pillar is holding this napkin," Bookman said, describing the proposal. "And I started crying."

She said yes and the two couldn't pay attention to the first half of the playoff game versus the Texas Rangers, as the couple alerted friends and family and soaked in what just happened. "I feel like if we'd paid more attention to the game, maybe they would have won," the groom-to-be said afterward.

Both Bookman, a teacher, and Stawychny, who works on movie sets, said one of the reasons the two connected is over their love of sports—especially the Jays.

Adapted from an article by Verity Stevenson first published in the *Toronto Star* on October 9, 2015.

Donaldson is the question mark. He passed concussion protocols, likely after sneaking back out to play the fifth inning, and at least one teammate said after the game, "He seemed fine."

Donaldson is expected to play game two but passing protocols doesn't mean he won't wake up on Friday with symptoms. He will be checked in the morning, and we'll see.

But even if Donaldson is out, the Jays still have the two best hitters in this series and, starting in game two, better starting pitchers. They can still win this thing. The last two months weren't an accident. These aren't the Leafs, or the Raptors.

"You know what? This is a deep team," said Pillar.

There's an old curse that gets ascribed to the Chinese, but whose actual origin is a mystery: May you live in interesting times.

Well, playoff baseball is back in Toronto and it's interesting as hell.

Game two goes tomorrow. Biggest game in 22 years, since the last one.

Jose Bautista is the one bright spot in the Blue Jays offense, homering in the sixth inning.

Rangers second baseman Rougned Odor is greeted by teammate Elvis Andrus after sealing the 5-3 Texas win with a seventh inning homer.

FIVE MOMENTS

DONALDSON GOES DOWN

Josh Donaldson lay on the turf for an uncomfortable few seconds after breaking up a potential double play with a hard slide into second base. Replays showed Donaldson's head striking the knee of the Rangers' second baseman Rougned Odor. Donaldson took the field in the fifth but then was removed. Manager John Gibbons said Donaldson passed all his initial concussion tests and will be reevaluated the next day.

PRICE'S DOUBLE PLUNKING

David Price hadn't hit a single batter since he joined the Jays at the trade deadline, but he plunked two on Thursday—the same guy twice, actually—hitting Odor to lead off both the third and fifth innings. In both cases Odor came around to score and those two runs proved to be the difference in the game. Price said later: "I got to pitch better."

Adapted from Five Moments by Brendan Kennedy first published by the *Toronto Star* on October 9, 2015.

ODOR'S HOMER

When he wasn't getting hit by pitches or colliding with the heads of star players, Texas second baseman Rougned Odor was causing trouble in other ways. He extended the Rangers' lead in the seventh inning with a frozen-rope homer to right field. The ball's exit velocity was tracked at 113 mph, putting it among the 100 fastest homers of the season.

SMOAK GOES DOWN SWINGING

The Jays couldn't muster much of anything against soft-tossing right-hander Yovani Gallardo but they had runners at the corners with two out in the fourth inning. Trailing 2-1, they needed a big knock from Justin Smoak but he whiffed badly on a slow curve to end the inning. It was Gallardo's only strikeout of the game.

BAUTISTA'S HOME RUN

Offering the home crowd a little something to cheer about, Jose Bautista hit his first career post-season home run in his first post-season game, sending a no-doubt drive to left field to lead off the sixth inning. The blast briefly drew the Jays within one of the Rangers' lead but not for long.

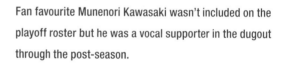

Fan favourite Munenori Kawasaki wasn't included on the playoff roster but he was a vocal supporter in the dugout through the post-season.

AL Division Series
GAME TWO

TORONTO BLUE JAYS 4 TEXAS RANGERS 6

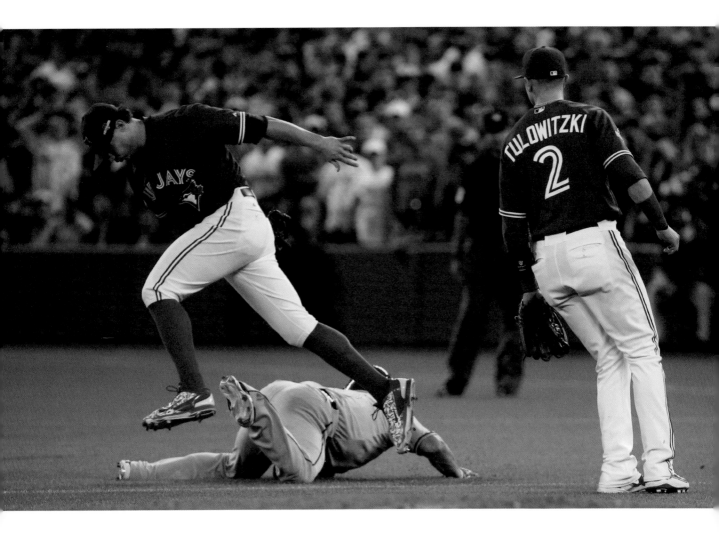

ROSIE DIMANNO *Toronto Star*
First published on October 10, 2015

TORONTO, ONTARIO—Texas Hold 'Em—cut the cards.

It's a tall hat order, rebounding from two-in-the-hole in a five-game series. But be reminded of this: The Blue Jays are not a team that folds.

And eight times before, the club that has lost the opening two games has rallied to win the best of a quintet.

Only two of those teams, however, have done so after dropping two games at home.

Further challenge: They'll have to do it without the crucial shut-down mojo of Brett Cecil, merely Toronto's most reliable reliever these past two months. Cecil tore a calf muscle in what looked like an otherwise innocuous run-down play that erased Mike Napoli trying to steal second in the eighth inning.

When last seen, a despondent Cecil was hobbling out

Reliever Brett Cecil suffers a torn calf muscle when he tags out Texas hitter Mike Napoli on a seemingly routine play.

of the clubhouse, his left leg encased in a walking cast.

"He got a tear where?" a stunned LaTroy Hawkins asked reporters afterwards. "Torn a calf? Oh, that hurts. Geezus. Wow. That's not good, that's not good at all.

"He's been our best pitcher since I've been here."

So there's that.

Adversity and attrition, jagged little pills. Still and yet, not a killer combination for so gaudily a gifted team. This is a club that absorbed the near-year injury absence of Marcus Stroman and the freak cracked scapula of Troy Tulowitzki down the stretch, some wobbly close-outs by Roberto Osuna of late and a starting ace who came undone in the first encounter of this series, to cite but a few of the bummers that have unfolded.

These are the cards you've been dealt, gentlemen. Move on.

But the Jays cannot continue to execute as poorly as they did against the Rangers in two contests at the Rogers Centre—0-for-home with game two's extra-innings' 6-4 defeat, the lengthiest playoff game in Toronto baseball history at an exhausting four hours and 57 minutes. (Felt longer.)

Rangers second baseman Rougned Odor appears to be caught off second base in the 14th inning but a replay rules that he is safe. The next batter, Hanser Alberto, singles and Odor dashes home, sliding past Jays catcher Russell Martin with the winning run.

They have been, frankly, unrecognizable, a mewling version of the prodigious outfit we've seen since the All-Star break and, particularly, post-trade deadline.

Yes, the officiating was scandalous yesterday, with a lazy eye strike zone from the home plate umpire.

Yes, probably, Troy Tulowitzki did tag out Toronto nemesis Rougned Odor—scrambling back to second—in the top of the 14th frame. Odor, the bane of Toronto's existence in this series, came 'round to score what proved to be the winning run, though Chris Gimenez added another for good measure.

That was three consecutive hits off the 40-year-old Hawkins, with the bullpen almost completely depleted and a sold-out crowd suddenly silenced.

Why manager John Gibbons didn't call earlier for the only relief arm he had left in Liam Hendriks—both Hawkins and Hendriks are right-handers, and the right-hitting Gimenez was at the dish—can be debated until the cows come home.

In what seemed a game without end, Gibbons likely wanted to keep one reliever in reserve should the innings just keep piling up.

But none of that explains why the Jays might not pass this way again in 2015.

Two measly hits off seven innings of Texas relief pitching tell the woeful tale.

Two measly hits from a club that led the majors in runs and extra base hits.

And one measly hit in extra innings, by Chris Colabello in the 12th frame, a leadoff single, with Dalton Pompey brought in to pinch-run. Pompey, utilizing his marvellous speed, stole second, stole third. But Russell Martin popped up, Kevin Pillar was whiffed looking and Ryan Goins hit a weak grounder.

"What did our bullpen give up—two hits, three hits?" countered Pillar.

FAST FACTS

The Blue Jays manage just two hitters in seven innings off five Texas relievers.

"We're good. We're not worried about it."

Jays pitcher **Marcus Stroman**

Six, actually. The first, from Cecil, scored Stroman's runner, tying the game 4-4. Then Osuna, Mark Lowe, Aaron Loup and Aaron Sanchez all went clean.

"Their bullpen's really good," Pillar continued. "Our bullpen is outstanding too. We just seemed unable to string together the hits or get that leadoff walk. C.C. had that big hit—I don't even know what inning, it all seems one long game. But we just didn't capitalize with that leadoff single. That was probably our best opportunity to score runs.

"Then, on the flip side, you see what they're able to do. They get a two-out base hit, an infield base hit and end up scoring two runs in the [14th] inning."

Bats gone weirdly quiet—save for Josh Donaldson's first-inning homer—could be blamed and the stingy pitching by the Texas 'pen can take a bow. But maybe if the Toronto hitters weren't all swinging for the fences—and Edwin Encarnacion did come within an eyelash of jacking a homer over the centre field wall in the 13th—perhaps the outcome would have been different.

No point autopsying what might have been.

In the event, Toronto has burned through its two strongest starters—Price, nowhere near his best on Thursday, and Stroman yesterday.

"We're good," Stroman assured the press afterwards. "We're not worried about it. We have a bunch of guys in this clubhouse who are unbelievably confident and we're just going to put this one behind and . . . focus on one game at a time, focus on the next one."

Well, that's the endlessly buoyant Stro' talking. But he'd looked just as glum in the dugout as every other Jay half an hour earlier, as the Rangers celebrated.

Reality bites hard, if not fatally, not yet.

"Back against the wall, obviously," said Tulowitzki.

"To lose two at home is not the way you want to start out a series. But since I've been around teams that make a run, they always have to answer something. So hopefully this will be ours—down 2-0, come back and win the series. It's not over."

FIVE MOMENTS

A SLOPPY START

The Jays were the most efficient team in base-ball at converting balls in play into outs in 2015, according to *Baseball Prospectus*, but they were very sloppy in the first inning. Delino DeShields led off with a long fly that popped out of Jose Bautista's glove. Prince Fielder's bouncer took a funny hop and eluded Ryan Goins. Russell Martin missed his throw to Josh Donaldson with Shin-Soo Choo caught in a rundown and Texas was up 2-0.

COLABELLO'S UNASSISTED DP

With the Jays reeling in the opening inning, first baseman Chris Colabello limited the damage with an unassisted double-play. With two on, one out and the Rangers already leading 2-0, he snared a weak grounder from Josh Hamilton, tagged him on the first-base line then ran across the diamond to also nab Prince Fielder between third and home.

ODOR SCORES AGAIN

Rougned Odor, the Rangers' second baseman and a persistent thorn in the Jays' side, scored twice. Odor drew a leadoff walk in the third and came around to score with some heads-up base running. He scampered from first to third on a high chopper to the mound. The speedy infielder then scored on a sacrifice fly to increase the Texas lead to 3-1.

CECIL GOES DOWN

The Jays lost their 4-3 lead in the eighth when Brett Cecil gave up a two-out single to Mike Napoli to drive in the speedy DeShields. Cecil then picked off Napoli at first and caught him in a rundown, but tore his left calf muscle. The injury ended his post-season.

REPLAY CONTROVERSY

In the 14th inning, right fielder Jose Bautista fielded a sharply hit single and tried to nab Odor, the lead runner, who had drifted past second base after moving up on the hit. Odor was back in time, but replays showed his right foot may have come off the bag for a brief moment as shortstop Troy Tulowitzki held the tag. Replay officials decided the play was inconclusive, the safe call on the field stood and Odor scored on the next play.

Adapted from Five Moments by Brendan Kennedy first published by the *Toronto Star* on October 10, 2015.

AL Division Series
GAME THREE

TORONTO BLUE JAYS 5   TEXAS RANGERS 1

RICHARD GRIFFIN *Toronto Star*
First published on October 12, 2015

ARLINGTON, TEXAS—The Blue Jays were simply looking for a hero on this night, someone to keep them from falling off the precipice of elimination, to step up and produce at key moments where the highest scoring team in baseball had failed in games one and two of the American League Division Series.

They found that hero in Troy Tulowitzki.

All the Jays wanted was to live to fight another day and that's what they earned the right to do, with a 5-1 victory in game three of the ALDS behind the subtle pitching of right-hander Marco Estrada and a clutch, three-run, two-out homer by Tulowitzki.

The Jays were nursing a nervous two-run lead in the sixth that would have been much higher, save for opportunities lost. Then they loaded the bases with nobody out

With the Blue Jays facing elimination, Marco Estrada puts his foot down and holds the Rangers to just five hits and one run.

and the Rangers quickly completed a first-to-home-to-first double play and it seemed their woes would continue.

Tulowitzki, who had just returned to action on the final weekend of the regular season against Tampa, had been hitless in the first two games of the series when he stepped in to face right-hander Chi Chi Gonzalez with Jose Bautista on third and Edwin Encarnacion on second.

With the count full, the intense Tulowitzki lined a pitch into the first few rows of the left field stands and the score was 5-0.

There must have been an audible sigh of relief in the Jays' dugout.

Tulowitzki was acquired from the Colorado Rockies as one of the top two-way shortstops in the game, but it was mostly defence that had helped the Jays to a 31-9 record when he was in the starting lineup.

"That was one of those big blows for us right there," third baseman Josh Donaldson said. "You know, I felt like we still should have scored some more runs out there tonight. A couple of base-running errors here or there, but it was nice to come out with the win tonight."

The Jays had chosen right-hander Marco Estrada for

"A do-or-die game, it doesn't surprise me he stepped up."

Manager **John Gibbons**

game three, with R.A. Dickey being handed the game four assignment.

Estrada joined the rotation in early May after rookie Daniel Norris was sent to the minors (and eventually traded to Detroit in the deal that brought David Price to Toronto).

Estrada went on to establish personal single-season highs in starts (28), wins (13) and innings pitched (181). He held hitters to a .203 average, leading the American League ahead of Houston's Dallas Keuchel.

In fact, of the four playoff starters in the playoff rotation, three were not there the first month. Estrada was in the bullpen, Marcus Stroman was injured and Price was with the Tigers.

 Estrada was in control through six innings, before allowing a couple of line-drive singles to the Rangers' Elvis Andrus and Josh Hamilton.

"It was unbelievable," Gibbons said.

"He's been doing that all year. A do-or-die game, it doesn't surprise me he stepped up. You could tell early in, he was on. We talked about guys with nerves or guys a little too emotional. How it would affect them. I didn't see that out of him at all."

Estrada was replaced by left-hander Aaron Loup after allowing just five hits over 88 pitches.

"I think Marco has proven to be an incredible asset for us in more ways than just pitching," said Dickey, the only member of the Jays' playoff rotation from opening day. "He's been so consistent in the clubhouse, you can count on him all the time. He works his tail off. It rubs off on the younger guys."

Loup pumped in strikes to his one batter, Rougned Odor, as a replacement in the role of the injured Brett Cecil. Odor grounded to Tulowitzki to drive in a run. Then right-hander Mark Lowe struck out catcher Robinson Chirinos to end the threat. Aaron Sanchez and Roberto Osuna closed out the game for Toronto.

The Jays opened the scoring for the first time in the series. Dioner Navarro laced a line drive that momentarily fooled Delino DeShields and one-hopped the wall, as the burly catcher trundled into second base. An infield single by Kevin Pillar to a diving Andrus placed runners at the corners for Ryan Goins. The second baseman grounded into a double play with Navarro scoring.

The Jays had a chance to put some distance between

Josh Donaldson celebrates his three-run home run with Jose Bautista after crossing the plate.

themselves and the Rangers in the fourth inning. Josh Donaldson led off with a double to right centre past a diving DeShields. Martin Perez walked Edwin Encarnacion intentionally with one out and then Chris Colabello and Tulowitzki also were issued bases-on-balls, with the latter forcing in a run. But Navarro grounded into a double play.

The television crew railed on about a balk by Perez that was not called by the umpires, with the bases loaded before the Navarro double play. That would have extended the lead.

The Jays continued to squander scoring opportunities in the fifth inning. Pillar grounded a single to centre that DeShields allowed to go through his legs.

Goins sacrificed him to third, then a soft broken-bat line drive by Ben Revere fooled Pillar and he was caught two-thirds of the way home.

FAST FACTS

Marco Estrada held hitters to a .203 batting average in 2015, leading the American League.

Troy Tulowitzki is congratulated by teammate Chris Colabello on his big three-run homer.

FIVE MOMENTS

NAVARRO OPENS SCORING

In his series debut, Jays catcher Dioner Navarro swung at the first pitch of the third inning, driving a long fly ball for a lead-off double. Navarro came around to score two batters later as Ryan Goins grounded into a double play. The early lead, while modest, at least put the Jays in the driver's seat and the Rangers on their heels.

ENCARNACION GETS FREE PASS

Josh Donaldson led off the fourth inning with a double and Rangers manager Jeff Banister opted to intentionally walk Edwin Encarnacion. The gambit failed as starting pitcher Martin Perez then seemed to lose the strike zone. He walked the next two batters, including Tulowitzki with the bases loaded, to hand the Jays their second run.

ESTRADA DISPELS ODOR

Jays starter Marco Estrada was dominant throughout, holding the Rangers off the board through the first six innings while limiting them to just three base runners. He was particularly sharp in two at-bats against pesky second baseman Rougned Odor, twice striking him out.

RALLY-KILLING DOUBLE PLAYS

The Jays put their leadoff runner aboard and moved him into scoring position in four straight innings. But on all four occasions the rallies were halted by double plays. When it happened again after Toronto loaded the bases with none out in the sixth, the Jays' fans were ready to throw up their hands. And then . . .

THE BREAKTHROUGH

Troy Tulowitzki's two-out, full-count, three-run home run in the sixth inning broke the game open for the Jays, affording some much-needed breathing room. It was also a breakthrough for Tulowitzki, who snapped a 0-for-11 post-season hitless streak with the long drive into left field.

Adapted from Five Moments by Brendan Kennedy first published by the *Toronto Star* on October 12, 2015.

AL Division Series
GAME FOUR

TORONTO BLUE JAYS 8 TEXAS RANGERS 4

"No lead is big enough."

Jays catcher **Russell Martin**

RICHARD GRIFFIN *Toronto Star*
First published on October 13, 2015

ARLINGTON, TEXAS—The only thing the Blue Jays wanted to accomplish when they arrived in Texas was to bring their American League Division Series back to Canada.

In game four at Globe Life Park, they utilized the home-run ball, their preferred weapon of mass destruction, and leaned on a pair of Cy Young winners—R.A. Dickey and David Price—to beat down the Rangers 8-4, evening the best-of-five ALDS at two games apiece.

"That was obviously our goal," third baseman Josh Donaldson said. "But still, if we lose [game five], we are still going home. We have to continue to play well and continue to do that at home, which we've done for the most part this year. We've just got to continue to play our best right now."

Kevin Pillar keeps the assembly line moving in the second inning with a solo shot to centre field and the Jays lead 4-0.

Price logged three innings of relief here, leaving Marcus Stroman in line to start game five and, if the Jays advance to the American League Championship Series, Marco Estrada to be the game one starter against either Kansas City or Houston. Price, Stroman and Dickey would follow Estrada.

Clearly, the team is living day to day.

The Jays, who led the majors in home runs this season, didn't wait long to take the lead in game four. They felt jumping out in front early would be essential in Texas and they scored first for the second straight game.

Leadoff hitter Ben Revere laid down a perfect bunt to open the game, dragging it past left-hander Derek Holland and out towards the second baseman for a hit.

Revere showed the importance of speed at the top of the lineup. Holland twice threw over to first base to keep him close, and then used a slide step to the plate. Donaldson drove the pitch—the fifth of the game—into the seats in right field for a 2-0 lead before anyone was out.

It was just what Gibbons had been hoping for. The home run by Donaldson was his second first-inning homer of the series and his 15th for the season, leading the Major League.

Edwin Encarnacion puts the Jays ahead 6-0 in the third inning, sliding home after a double by Chris Colabello.

"If you could script it, that's the way you would want," Donaldson said. "Give R.A. a little bit of breathing room right there, right off the bat. That's just kind of how we [have] played up to this point, and it was nice to come out today and do that."

Two outs later, first baseman Chris Colabello hit his first post-season home run, also to the opposite field. In the second, Kevin Pillar extended the lead to four runs with a home run that sailed into the bullpen in left field and was caught by Price.

The Jays' ace was loosening up with Stroman in case either man was needed in relief of Dickey.

"I didn't see him catch it, but when I went out there he told me he had it and I was able to get it authenticated," Pillar said. "It's pretty special to get your first post-season home run, especially under the circumstances with our back against the wall. Yeah, that was pretty cool."

It marked the first time that the Jays had hit three home runs in any post-season game.

Gibbons surprised many in the bottom of the fifth when, with Toronto leading by six runs, he lifted Dickey from the game, just one out shy of his first post-season win in his first start, at the age of 40. Price, who had warmed up in game three and was now pitching in long relief, replaced him.

Dickey was disappointed, but the fact that it was the club's starting ace softened what was a blow to his competitive psyche.

"Just a manager's decision," catcher Russell Martin said.

"We're trying to win games. I definitely believe Dickey can get [Shin-Soo Choo] out, but you can't fault [Gibbons] for having a lefty-on-lefty matchup and one pitch later the guy's out, so good call. In the post-season, not much is surprising to me."

"You try and get outs, however you can get 'em. No lead is big enough."

The Jays have done well to come back from a two-game deficit to force an ultimate loser-go-home game.

Historically, there have been 73 previous five-game series in which one team had a 2-1 advantage in games. The trailing team in those series went 36-37 in game four. Of the 36 winners that tied the series, 13 of those had, like the Jays, been down 0-2. Eight of those 13 went on to win game five.

"Our mindset the whole time has been you've got to win three games," Pillar said. "It doesn't matter how you do it, what order you do it in, but it's definitely nice flying home knowing we've got another game in Toronto.

"I would imagine they were looking forward to closing out at home. But we saw what they did to win the division. They lost some big games in the stretch and were able to respond. If anything, they have confidence. They won two games in Toronto and we didn't win any games. Momentum out the window. It's going to be who goes out and plays better."

The Jays have won nine of their last 10 post-season road games, but still have not won a home game at the Rogers Centre since Joe Carter touched 'em all back in 1993.

FAST FACTS

The Blue Jays have won nine of their last 10 post-season road games.

With the Jays ahead 7-1, R.A. Dickey is pulled in the fifth inning—just one out short of his first post-season win.

FIVE MOMENTS

FAST START

Jays outfielder Ben Revere was safe on a drag bunt to open the game and third baseman Donaldson slammed the next pitch into the right field stands to give Toronto a 2-0 lead. Two batters later, Chris Colabello also homered and the Blue Jays were off and running.

DICKEY SHARP

R.A. Dickey made the first post-season start of his career and held Texas in check as the Jays built a 7-1 lead. Kevin Pillar went deep in the third, giving Toronto three homers in a game for the first time in their playoff history. Dickey continued to roll along, allowing just one run on five hits.

PRICE IN RELIEF

With Dickey cruising and two out in the fifth inning, Jays manager John Gibbons popped out of the dugout, strolled to the mound and summoned left ace David Price from the bullpen. Price retired Shin-Soo Choo on the first pitch and allowed three runs over three innings of work to receive credit for the win.

THE MANAGER

Blue Jays manager John Gibbons admitted later that the decision to pull Dickey was "probably not a relationship-building move. But a team win, that's what I was looking for . . . You know what? Things happen fast. And sometimes, I've learned, I've watched enough baseball games—sometimes the only chance you've got to win is to keep the team from coming back."

THE ROTATION

With Price, who was slated to be the starter for game five, being used in relief, Marcus Stroman will get the ball in the deciding game of the series. And if the Jays win game five, Marco Estrada will be first up against either Houston or Kansas City in the opening game of the American League Championship Series.

Adapted from a segment by Brendan Kennedy first published on Star Touch on October 13, 2015.

AL Division Series
GAME FIVE

TORONTO BLUE JAYS 6 TEXAS RANGERS 3

BRUCE ARTHUR *Toronto Star*
First published on October 15, 2015

TORONTO, ONTARIO—You will remember the seventh inning, above all. You will laugh about it with your friends over beers, order another round, what the hell. You will still find it hard to believe, and will have to reassure yourself. You will remember the waves of emotion, the anger and the despair, and then that feeling. You know, the big one. That sound. The crack.

"When he started his swing, I was real hopeful, because I knew he was going to hit it hard," said pitcher R.A. Dickey. "And I was halfway on the carpet before the ball ever left the field."

Yes, you will remember this.

Umpire Dale Scott calls "no play" after Russell Martin's routine throw back to the mound clips the hand of Shin-Soo Choo in the batter's box and rolls toward third base.

Until that moment, it felt biblical. Game five of Toronto's first playoff series in 22 years, against the Texas Rangers, was tied 2-2, a tense game, a nerves game.

With a man on third, Jays catcher Russell Martin went to throw the ball back to the pitcher. Rangers right fielder Shin-Soo Choo was stretching out his left arm and adjusting his elbow pad. The throw hit the bat. The man on third, Rougned Odor, came home.

It stood as the winning run. You couldn't decide a series on that play, could you? Imagine that. It was the right call. But oh, Lord.

Chaos. Beers came cartwheeling out of the stands onto the field, or into the crowd. One reportedly hit a baby, and another one whizzed by John Gibbons. A lot of Toronto fans should have been embarrassed, ejected and arrested. The boos thundered, and it was a maelstrom, mayhem, a meltdown, a mess. Some of us should have done better.

In the Jays dugout, Mark Buehrle was ejected. After an 18-minute delay it was still the seventh inning, and when the Jays got out of it that exhausted cheerful old theme song played, "OK Blue Jays," that completed the descent into dystopian anarchical farce.

Jose Bautista flips his bat after the series-winning home run: "I still don't know how I did it."

And then . . .

"Like a novel that you don't want to put down, you know?" said Dickey.

I mean, really. What do you say? Martin came to the plate, and he was desperate.

"I'm thinking, I better do something," Martin said. "I need to get on base here. I better do something. I mean, I knew what I did."

He hit a dribbler, and ran. "I haven't been down the line that hard [this year]. I [thought], I've got to do something."

The Rangers booted it. Then the next one. And the next. When Josh Donaldson blooped a ball that barely cleared Odor's glove, brushing it, suddenly the game was tied.

"I was pretty pissed at what I just did," Donaldson said. "Bases loaded, one out, and I get sawed off like that."

And with men at the corners and two outs and a 1-1 count and the building on its feet, Jose Bautista smashed a 97 mph fastball 442 feet to left, a rocket, gone.

He stood there, 34 years old, and he watched it go and looked at the pitcher and flipped his bat aside like a king, majestic. They may erect a statue of that bat flip. It was the biggest home run in this building in 22 years, and you will tell your friends about it, and you will laugh in disbelief, years from now. Holy bleep, you'll say. The sound was a crack, whole and pure, and then the end of the world.

"I've never seen a stadium so alive," said Martin. "Ever. I can't describe it. I can definitely remember it. I can still see it. One of the greatest moments of my life."

"I can't really remember what was going through my mind, to be quite honest with you," said Bautista. "After I made contact, I just, you know—I didn't plan anything I did. And so I still don't know how I did it."

"The game of baseball, if you try to figure it out, you'll drive yourself crazy," said Donaldson, soaked in champagne, his blue eyes a little spacey. "I mean, you look at what happened, there are a lot of crazy people out

FAST FACTS

It's only the third time in 81 attempts that a team has lost the first two games at home and come back to win a five-game series.

"One of the greatest moments of my life."

Catcher **Russell Martin**

there." Of Bautista, he said, "The guy's amazing. He's my hero . . . I want to hug him forever."

All the runs were unearned, unless you were speaking cosmically.

There was more, but the seventh inning is what you will remember.

When it ended, general manager Alex Anthopoulos and his men sprayed water bottles everywhere, and then he sped out and got to the hallway, and his wife, Cristina, appeared in the doorway and she screamed, just screamed, and they collided in an embrace, and his two toddling children pulled their father down as their mother screamed again. In the clubhouse, the Jays sprayed the champagne again, and lit the cigars again, and will live to play another day.

You will remember this. They will, too.

Josh Donaldson sprays his teammates with champagne as the post-game celebration spills onto the field at the Rogers Centre.

FIVE MOMENTS

GOINS' RUN-SAVING SNAG

The homers will get the glory, but the Jays also won with defence. Kevin Pillar stole a hit from Josh Hamilton in the fourth, running and diving headlong to make the catch. And then Ryan Goins make a sliding snag on Andrus' would-be RBI grounder up the middle. That bailed out Stroman and kept the Jays within one in the sixth.

ENCARNACION'S PARROT TROT

With the Jays back in the dugout after Goins' run-saving play, Edwin Encarnacion stepped to the plate with one out in the sixth and crushed Cole Hamels' first pitch off the facing of the upper deck to tie the game at 2-2.

CONTROVERSY ERUPTS

With the game still tied and the Rangers' Rougned Odor at third base, Jays catcher Russell Martin's routine throw back to pitcher Aaron Sanchez ricocheted off Shin-Soo Choo's outstretched hand as he stood in the batter's box. Odor ran home on the play but home-plate umpire Dale Scott called time. After a replay appeal, the run counted.

RANGERS FALL APART

Following the chaos and confusion of the top of the seventh inning, the Rangers returned to the field twitchy and tense. They made three straight errors to start the bottom of the seventh inning as the Jays loaded the bases against Hamels with none out.

BAUTISTA'S BLAST

Pillar said it was the biggest home run hit in Toronto since Joe Carter's World Series walk-off in 1993, and he's right. Bautista's game-winning, three-run bomb in the seventh inning—after everything that had happened leading up to it—was among the biggest hits in Blue Jays history. The brazen slugger's subsequent bat flip was just as epic.

Adapted from Five Moments by Brendan Kennedy first published by the *Toronto Star* on October 15, 2015.

AL Championship Series
GAME ONE

TORONTO BLUE JAYS 0   KANSAS CITY ROYALS 5

ROSIE DIMANNO *Toronto Star*
First published October 17, 2015

KANSAS CITY—It was a game that should have had a manufacturer's label affixed to it.

As in: Manufactured by.

Which is how the Royals usually score their runs—in singles and doubles, with speed, exploiting small slivers of opportunity, pouncing.

If you like your baseball in canapé morsels.

Which worked so well for Kansas City in the regular season, nudging them in unspectacular fashion to first overall among the American League brethren.

Which worked so well versus Houston in the AL Division Series, where the Royals weren't the dominant team, not by a long shot, but did emerge as survivors.

Which worked well enough in the opening game of the American League Championship Series to build up an early 2-0 lead over Toronto while the Jays were still

Royals pitcher Edinson Volquez shuts out the Jays for six innings.

looking for their first hit of the evening against starter Edinson Volquez despite smacking the Dominican quite hard all over the field.

It certainly wasn't either clever or overpowering pitching from Volquez that kept the gaudy Jays lineup from doing its typical big-bop stuff, inning after inning after inning—a post-season absence of offence that likewise almost brought the team to ruin in their division series against the Texas Rangers, until the bats finally woke up.

Under a midnight blue Kansas sky, however, the bats rolled over and slumbered, snoozing while the Royals knocked off a snappy 5-0 win in game one of the ALCS.

A microcosm of what ailed the visitors was evident in the events of the sixth inning, when the Jays forced Volquez to throw 37 pitches—and that would be it for Volquez, as it turned out, all pooped out and worn down after throwing a total of 111 pitches for the evening, and walking four.

Two of those walks were allowed in that sixth frame: Lead-off hitter Josh Donaldson aboard on nine pitches, Jose Bautista also given a stroll on nine pitches. So two runners on, nobody out, Edwin Encarnacion at the dish, just the scenario manager John Gibbons might have hoped for.

A glum Troy Tulowitzki strikes out in the sixth inning with two runners on base and two out, ending the Jays' best chance to score.

But E.E. struck out looking, Chris Colabello lined out to left field and Troy Tulowitzki was also punched out without taking the wood off his shoulders on the seventh pitch of that at-bat.

Nothing to show for any of it, a ripe opportunity to get themselves back before Kansas City manager Ned Yost had the chance to call upon his outstanding dominant bullpen, an area where the Royals enjoy a significant edge over Toronto.

Tulowitzki, apart from his heroic jack in game four against the Rangers, has largely continued his hitting blues into the post-season. For playing at all, with a recently cracked scapula, he gets a pass. And his defence had been, in the main, trademark sharp, including a marvellous 4-6-3 double-play.

But these long lapses in Toronto hitting, where they have trouble wringing out a measly single with men on base, are mystifying. They're also becoming a worrisome trend in the post-season.

Volquez was nowhere near masterful yet the Jays—so lethal with the bats in the regular season, dominating nearly every offensive category—could get no more than two hits off him through six, nothing at all till the fourth, and certainly never came close to mounting a threat.

Balls hit hard were mostly hit directly at the Royals, with no counter to the shift except from Ryan Goins of all people, with his first hit of the playoffs in the fifth, smacked sharply up the middle, to no avail. Kauffman Stadium is no hitter-friendly Rogers. So they don't build their teams to crank homers.

They don't bash, they knick and saw and turn the lathe. They are Bob the Builder–like. Un-bashing, un-dashing. Nowhere near as exciting as a year ago, from wild card to seven-game-stretch World Series.

Toronto manager John Gibbons, who was the bench coach here for three years between Blue Jays engagements (and a brief dip into Double-A ball), saw it coming, in a fashion, several hours before the Royals tucked game one of the American League Championship Series into their back pocket.

"For the most part, they're a free-swinging team. They put the ball in play. They probably manufacture runs better than anybody in baseball."

That's certainly how the Royals got to Toronto starter Marco Estrada in the early going, making the most out of not very much—a lead-off double by Alex Gordon in the third, then, one strike-out later and back around the top of the order, a stand-up double by Alcides Escobar, his second of the night, which brought Gordon in to score the Royals' first run. Followed shortly thereafter by a base hit single the other way from Lorenzo Cain, cashing in a big two-out run, up 2-0.

The only major mistake Estrada committed in his 5⅓ innings of work was a fastball down the middle of the plate in the fourth, which Salvador Perez drilled over the wall in left, which made it 3-0. And so it went.

Perhaps the Jays were messed up in the head, first time in a week they were playing a game and not facing elimination.

Better snap out of the hitting doldrums soon or they'll be back in that twisted sphincter spot.

Jays starter Marco Estrada reflects on his performance after being pulled with one out in the sixth. He allows just six hits but gets no run support.

FIVE MOMENTS

LEADOFF MAGIC

Royals leadoff hitter Alcides Escobar swings at Marco Estrada's first pitch of the game and sends it down the left-field line for a double. According to "Esky Magic," when Escobar swings at the first pitch, the Royals are 43-17 this season. Now they're 44-17.

DOUBLES POWER

Royals left fielder Alex Gordon leads off the third inning by hooking Estrada's pitch down the right-field line and scores the opening run two batters later when Escobar also doubles. Escobar promptly scores on a single by Lorenzo Cain as Kansas City takes an early 2-0 lead.

PEREZ GOES YARD

Royals catcher Sal Perez adds to the Royals' lead in the fourth inning when he sends Estrada's first-pitch fastball over the deep left-centre wall at Kauffman Stadium.

VOLQUEZ FREEZES BAUTISTA

Meanwhile, Royals starter Edinson Volquez is dealing all night. He might be at his best in the fourth inning, when he leads off with a three-pitch strikeout to Jose Bautista. The Jays slugger doesn't lift the bat off his shoulder.

BATTLING

Josh Donaldson and Bautista draw back-to-back walks to open the sixth inning, but with the potential tying run at the plate, Volquez retires Edwin Encarnacion, Chris Colabello and Troy Tulowitzki. The Jays battle Volquez for a combined 37 pitches, but don't score.

Adapted from Five Moments by Brendan Kennedy first published by the *Toronto Star* on October 17, 2015.

AL Championship Series
GAME TWO

TORONTO BLUE JAYS 3 KANSAS CITY ROYALS 6

"I thought that I heard something."

Jays infielder **Ryan Goins**

BRUCE ARTHUR *Toronto Star*
First published October 18, 2015

KANSAS CITY—So Ryan Goins saw a ghost, or heard one, and that's where it started. Maybe you can blame the ghost.

With nearly 40,000 Kansas City fans screaming at him, Goins was chasing a pop-up when he thought he heard a scrap on the wind: I got it. Except, he didn't. The ball dropped, and the bottom fell out of the Toronto Blue Jays right after that. If you want to blame Goins, go ahead, because he does.

"I thought late that I heard something," said Goins after a shocking 6-3 loss to the Kansas City Royals in game two of the American League Championship Series. "And it wasn't . . ."

He trailed off, sort of. But that wasn't why the Blue Jays lost. It's not why this team is in a 0-2 hole. It was a

Ryan Goins calls for a pop-up but then pulls up and lets the ball fall between him and Jose Bautista. The miscue opens the door for a Royals comeback.

factor, a butterfly flapping its wings, but there were other winds blowing, too. This wasn't the Texas Rangers making three straight errors. This was a team getting beat.

"One small mistake opened the door for them," said Toronto right fielder Jose Bautista, tight-lipped and clearly angry. "We're a great team, we're playing good baseball, and today was just one of those days where a small mistake can open the door for another team. So we're not going to over-analyze it."

It was a screw-up, sure. Bautista said he didn't hear anybody shout anything, and there was no confusion, and Goins said he couldn't have heard one voice in the crowd with all that noise, so it's a mystery.

Except that after Goins screwed up there was a man on first and no outs in a 3-0 game in which Toronto's starting pitcher, David Price, had been a merciless, vengeful god for six innings. Until he wasn't.

"I don't think I struggled," said Price, who was tagged with his record-tying seventh consecutive post-season loss. "It's frustrating, but I didn't struggle."

Yes, and no. Through six innings Price had allowed three balls to be hit out of the infield, and had retired

"I just gave up hits at the wrong time."

Jays starter **David Price**

18 batters in a row. Finally, after so many strangely rough playoff outings, he was himself again. He needed just 66 pitches to get through six innings, and you thought, this is why you pay this man his money, or somebody else does. That playoff monkey on his back was getting flung into orbit. David Price wasn't screwing around.

And then the ghost yelled, but everything after that was earned. A Lorenzo Cain single, opposite field. An Eric Hosmer single, 3-1, no outs. A Hosmer hit-and-run as Kendry Morales grounded out, taking away a potential double play ball, and it was 3-2.

Price was still making pitches, but they were getting hit. Mike Moustakas, single, and Bautista's throw to the plate was wide, 3-3. Alex Gordon, double to the gap, on a two-seam fastball that ran towards the middle, the one pitch Price said he would have liked to have back. 4-3.

"Their at-bats, they were able to fight tough pitches off and really find a way to scrap away some hits," said Jays catcher Russell Martin. "There weren't many well-struck baseballs. They'd seen his cutters and changeup, and they just fought them off until they found a pitch they could do something with."

But Price didn't put them away, the way he had for six one-hit innings. Even Alex Rios managed a single to make it 5-3. Price threw 66 pitches in six innings, and 30 in the seventh. The floor gave way.

"I just gave up hits at the wrong time," said Price. "I felt good. That's a pretty scrappy team, and they continued to battle, again and again. Good things are going to happen. I know it."

FAST FACTS

Jays starter David Price retired 18 hitters in a row and threw just 66 pitches over the first six innings.

Mayors bet on it

Toronto Mayor John Tory and his Kansas City counterpart have their own showdown on the eve of the American League Championship Series.

Mayor Sly James posts a YouTube video ribbing Tory, saying his Royals will beat the Blue Jays.

If the Royals lose, he offers, "We will send you a selection of three different barbecue restaurants' ribs and their sauces." K.C. barbecue, he boasts, is the best in the U.S.

But, he adds, "I wouldn't start getting your knives and forks out, however, because we plan to win this thing . . . Make it somethin' good, brother. We have our own maple syrup, so something else maybe."

Tory, a lawyer who clearly enjoys the fun parts of politics, responds by marching into Nathan Phillips Square carrying a Jose Bautista bat.

Artfully arranged between the T and the O in the Toronto sign sit several kinds of Toronto-brewed craft beer, maple syrup, and other treats he says he'll give James no matter who wins.

"I think it's very important that if they eat all that barbecue down there, they should have something to wash it down, and I think it is time that people in Kansas City, up to and including the mayor, have a chance for the first time in their lives to drink some real beer," Tory says.

That beer, he adds, "will come with the recognition—that will come on their part very quickly indeed—that not only are our hitters stronger, not only are our pitchers stronger, but our craft beer is much stronger too. So don't get carried away, Mayor James, on the beer, that is. We're going to look forward to receiving that barbecue. And go Jays!"

Adapted from an article by David Rider first published in the Toronto Star *on October 17, 2015.*

He needs to say that, maybe. David Price isn't a lousy playoff pitcher, but he has done some lousy pitching in the playoffs.

You can say manager John Gibbons left him in too long, but Price's pitch count was still reasonable, and it's becoming clear that Gibbons doesn't much trust his bullpen outside of Aaron Sanchez and Roberto Osuna. You can say the Goins error opened the gates, but the Royals got five more legitimate hits after that. Price didn't blame Goins. Price just got beat.

"It happens," said Price. "It's probably going to happen again. You've got to be able to move forward, and I didn't do a good job of that."

Baseball can change so fast, and it can change back, and this series is a long way from over. People will blame Price, and Goins, and Gibbons, sure. But beneath all that, this Toronto team has scored three runs in two games, and that allows the little things to become enormous.

Ryan Goins heard a ghost, and David Price continues to be haunted by one.

Jose Bautista crouches in disbelief after he is called out on strikes in the seventh inning of game two.

FIVE MOMENTS

MARTIN STYMIED

With runners at first and second and just one out in the second inning, Blue Jays catcher Russell Martin lines a fastball up the middle but is robbed by a diving Alcides Escobar, the Royals shortstop, who steals a would-be RBI from Martin and flips the ball to Ben Zobrist at second base to double off Edwin Encarnacion and end the inning.

TULO SNAPS SLUMP

Jays shortstop Troy Tulowitzki, who is still feeling the effects of his cracked shoulder blade, has a good day at the plate, going 2-for-2 with an RBI double to snap a 0-for-13 hitless streak. "I'm just battling, just trying to do what I can," he says.

PRICE STRIKES OUT SIDE

Jays starter David Price is at his best in the sixth inning when he strikes out the side. He mixes and matches all of his pitches—alternating his 79 mph curveball, 91 mph cutter, 85 mph changeup, and 94 mph fastball—to keep Alex Gordon, Alex Rios and Alcides Escobar guessing.

THE SKY FALLS

The Royals' Ben Zobrist leads off the seventh inning with a pop-up to shallow right field. Blue Jays second baseman Ryan Goins looks set to catch it, repeatedly waving off right fielder Jose Bautista. But at the last second, Goins gives way and the ball drops in for a hit. He says later that he thought he heard an "I got it," perhaps amid the crowd noise.

GAME-OVER GORDON

Outfielder Alex Gordon has the biggest hit of the Royals' seventh-inning rally, drilling a David Price fastball into the right field gap to knock in the winning run. Later, Gordon says the dropped fly ball was the opening Kansas City needed against Price.

Adapted from Five Moments by Brendan Kennedy first published by the *Toronto Star* on October 18, 2015.

One bright spot in the Blue Jays lineup is Troy Tulowitzki, who breaks out of a mini-slump with two hits, including an RBI double.

AL Championship Series
GAME THREE

TORONTO BLUE JAYS 11 KANSAS CITY ROYALS 8

BRUCE ARTHUR *Toronto Star*
First published October 20, 2015

TORONTO, ONTARIO—John Gibbons charted the course before the festivities, before the blowout, before the whole thing turned into a party for one side, and not the other.

"For us, personally, we need to score anyway," said the Toronto Blue Jays manager. "That's kind of who we are."

The Kansas City Royals won the first two games of the American League Championship Series with pitching and scrapping and magic, and they made the Jays look small and cold. And then they came to Toronto, and the Jays came heavy. No matter what, one of these teams is going to be hard to bury. Grab your shovel, but be ready to fight.

Jays centre fielder Kevin Pillar adds to his archive of highlight reel plays when he catches a first-inning drive off the bat of Lorenzo Cain and crashes into the wall.

And that's as it should be. In game three the Jays played like themselves, like their best selves. They pounded the ball to places the Royals couldn't chase it down unless they bought a ticket. They talked about how they needed an early lead, before Kansas City's near-death bullpen got one. They talked about breaking out.

Hey, welcome home. Troy Tulowitzki, who was waving at balls early in game two, hit a three-run home run to centre, 411 feet.

Josh Donaldson, with one hit in his last three games, sent a two-run homer to left centre, 400 feet.

Ryan Goins, who looked eviscerated as he answered question after question about his bizarre game-two gaffe, added a solo shot to right centre, 392 feet. He had a nice night, Goins. He deserved that.

"That's what we do," said Gibbons.

But two of those homers may not have gone out in the cold air of Kauffman Stadium, with its 410-foot centre field fence, to 400 in Toronto. In Toronto, they go. It was almost enough to make you wonder about the end of the regular season, and the failure to secure four games here, rather than the middle three.

"I felt like we had great at-bats the entire night."

Jays third baseman **Josh Donaldson**

But in the meantime, they needed it all to win this game. The Jays needed to pack it on, to keep running, to keep swinging. They needed to push the lead to 9-2, 10-4, 11-4. Because in the ninth the Royals started stringing together hits, and the Jays were forced to go to closer Roberto Osuna, who may have a cracked nail or a blister on his throwing hand, and therefore no slider, according to ESPN Deportes.

But they held, because four ninth-inning runs weren't enough. They won 11-8, because they had a cushion. These are the Toronto Blue Jays. Series ain't over.

"I felt like we had great at-bats the entire night," said Donaldson. "And we were able to go get that big hit for us, and I've always said the run is the hardest at playoff time. And we're going to have to come out tomorrow and play just as good if not better, because you see the quality of team they have over there. They don't stop until the 27th out. They're tough."

This is what the Jays are facing. They are facing a team whose starting pitcher in game one, Edinson Volquez, junked the plan to throw inside because he, in his words, "felt sexy," and decided to throw a pile of the best pitches of his life to the outer half of the plate instead.

They are facing a team that starts a human hashtag named Alcides Escobar at leadoff even though it doesn't make any sense, that strings together hits, that chases down what you hit like Rafael Nadal in his prime, and forces you to hit it better, hit it again. The Royals are baseball in its weirdly mystical sense, all in all.

Josh Donaldson celebrates after cracking a two-run homer in the third inning to put the Blue Jays ahead 9-2. It turns out to be the game-winning hit after the Royals rally. Final score 11-8.

Royals starter Johnny Cueto seems rattled by the Rogers Centre crowd as he gives up eight runs before being pulled with no one out in the third inning.

The Jays are baseball with a club, and a bigger club, and after leaving 18 men on base in the first two games of this series, they were due for something like this. They needed this because going down 0-3 would be something close to the end, and because they needed a big enough lead that the Royals couldn't come back. They got it.

The Jays came back to a changed city. They didn't let the plebes in the 500s buy tall boys they could throw, but they could have, because nobody was throwing anything on this night. Someone brought a sign that said "We're Not in Kansas Anymore," which must have been funny to the people of Kansas City, Missouri. It turned into a party, and it never really stopped.

If the Toronto Blue Jays do lose this series, they can blame the weather in Baltimore, the beer and the champagne, Osuna's second blown save, and themselves. If it comes to that, then maybe they will rue the final few days of the season, and wish they had four possible games in this giant concrete pinball machine, and look back with regret.

But that's not on the menu yet, and may never be. Right now, the Jays are back. They're not in Kansas anymore, but then, they never were.

FAST FACTS

The Jays score six runs in the bottom of the third inning to tie a team record for the post-season.

Second baseman Ryan Goins comes up big with a key two-run single to put the Jays ahead 2-1 in the second inning and then seals the win with a solo homer in the fifth.

FIVE MOMENTS

TOUGH START FOR STROMAN

Monday marked the third time in as many post-season starts that Marcus Stroman gave up an extra-base hit to start the game. In this case it was a leadoff triple to Alcides Escobar that would have likely just been a single if Jose Bautista didn't misplay it. Stroman wasn't fooling the Royals. He gave up 11 hits—his highest total of the season—and garnered just three swing-and-misses from the Royals' aggressive hitters.

HUMAN HIGHLIGHT REEL

With Jays great Devon White in attendance to throw out the first pitch on Monday night, Kevin Pillar did his best impression of the speedy centre fielder in the first inning, racing back to the warning track and reaching out to rob Lorenzo Cain of extra bases before crashing into the centre field wall. The moment was key in that it settled things down for Stroman.

ROUGH RIDE FOR CUETO

The sold-out crowd of 49,751 was all over Royals right-hander Johnny Cueto with chants of "CUE-TO! CUE-TO!" Jays fans must have been aware of the 2013 National League wild-card game when the Pittsburgh Pirates' crowd noticeably rattled Cueto, then pitching for the Cincinnati Reds. The razzing seemed to work again this night as Cueto surrendered eight earned runs.

REMOVE THOSE HORNS

The distance from goat to hero is often very short in sports, and Ryan Goins proved that in game three. The Jays second baseman, who dropped a routine pop-up that ignited a five-run Royals rally in game two, put Toronto on the board in the second inning with a go-ahead, two-run single. The hit came after a remarkable nine-pitch battle, in which Goins fouled off three of Cueto's pitches and worked the count full before poking a single the other way.

THE BIG INNING

With Cueto on the ropes after the Jays sent eight to the plate in their three-run second inning, they delivered a knockout blow with a six-run, bat-around third. Edwin Encarnacion led off with a single, Chris Colabello walked and Troy Tulowitzki hit his second three-run homer of the post-season to straightaway centre field. Russell Martin walked and Kevin Pillar doubled him home before Josh Donaldson slammed a two-run homer.

Adapted from Five Moments by Brendan Kennedy first published by the *Toronto Star* on October 20, 2015.

AL Championship Series
GAME FOUR

TORONTO BLUE JAYS 2 KANSAS CITY ROYALS 14

"I don't want to go home yet."

Catcher **Russell Martin**

BRUCE ARTHUR *Toronto Star*
First published October 21, 2015

TORONTO, ONTARIO—Russell Martin thrust his hands in his pockets and he smiled, but not all the way. When the Toronto Blue Jays needed to win three elimination games against Texas, their catcher had cheerfully told his teammates they just needed to win 11 in a row again. He was reminded of this. He liked that.

"I mean, it's the same situation, backs against the wall, win or go home, and I don't want to go home yet," said Martin, after the Jays were crushed 14-2 by the Kansas City Royals on Tuesday, and now trail 3-1 in the American League Championship Series.

"I love this team. I love our fight. We've shown our ability to come back before. Obviously, it's a different team. I definitely think Kansas City is better than Texas,

A dejected Kevin Pillar sits on the grass during another pitching change as the Royals pound out 15 hits against six Blue Jays pitchers.

so it's going to be a tougher battle. It's a challenge. I'm up to the challenge."

If you have learned anything about this team, you know that they can do this. These Toronto Blue Jays should be written off when they lose the last game, and not before. They can do this.

But after four games the Royals are a better team in every way. Every one. You can say it could have been different, and should have been different, but it's not. This isn't the end, but you can see it from here.

"We're going to have to play our best game in order to beat these guys," said third baseman Josh Donaldson.

They haven't done that. The Jays haven't gotten a signature performance from a starter in this series, though David Price came maddeningly close. In this game, they couldn't mash the biggest fly ball pitcher in baseball. And they finally had a starter blow up, and had to rummage through the dusty and disused end of their bullpen, until infielder Cliff Pennington became the first position player to pitch in a playoff game in Major League Baseball history. It could have been worse. He didn't give up a run.

With the bullpen battered and beaten, Jays manager John Gibbons turns to utility infielder Cliff Pennington to come in and record the final out.

The day started with Royals pitcher Johnny Cueto, through his teammate Edinson Volquez, accusing the Jays of stealing signs from centre field in game three, the old Man-in-White legend. Even if it wasn't a ridiculous idea, it was pretty roundly disproved on this day.

"I mean, honestly, I would tell you," Martin said. "We did it with the Yankees, we don't do it here. We just f---ing hit, man. We f---ing crush. Whether it's here, or on the road or whatever. We don't do it. Maybe it's because they do it, and they're projecting."

If the Kansas City Royals are projecting, then that may be why they are hitting, sort of crushing, merciless. They are hitting .331 in the series, and they are close to taking everything.

Little things add up to big things. R.A. Dickey was pulled from game four of the Texas series because manager John Gibbons doesn't trust the knuckleball. And on this day, it floated like a balloon and the Royals counted off as many of the different kinds of at-bats as they could: bunt single, homer, walk, stolen base, regular single, passed ball, 4-3 groundout, sac fly and finally a strikeout.

It was 5-0 when Dickey was removed. It was only 5-2 after Liam Hendricks was dragged out and held the line for as long as he could, going to the seventh. It's easy to forget that, now. They were one three-run homer away.

And then, the problem. Gibbons is managing his bullpen like it's full of explosives, and he's proving himself right. For some reason, he chose 42-year-old LaTroy Hawkins, who had been lit up like a Vegas casino in his two playoff appearances, and who loaded the bases with no outs in the seventh.

Gibbons pulled out Ryan Tepera from the spot that could have been Mark Buehrle, because Brett Cecil is hurt and Aaron Loup had to leave for a family matter, and the Jays wanted to save Aaron Sanchez and Roberto Osuna for a game five.

Gibbons could have gone with Mark Lowe, but he didn't, until the eighth. That's why Pennington got to flash his fastball, and his curve. The Royals have scored 22 runs in two games here, and the Jays are getting beaten. The game two collapse is looming larger all the time.

I won't rule out this team until the last out, and neither should you. They will rely on Marco Estrada to save their season on Wednesday, with the back of the bullpen a smoking ruin, and will hope to get to David Price in game six and Marcus Stroman in game seven. It ain't over 'til it's over, Yogi Berra was said to say.

He's right. It ain't over. But it's close.

FAST FACTS

The Royals have scored 22 runs in the first two games in Toronto.

Ryan Goins, Chris Colabello, Russell Martin and R.A. Dickey look for relief from a scoreboard replay but nothing will save them on this day.

FIVE MOMENTS

PESKY ESKY

Royals shortstop Alcides Escobar surprised the Jays in the first inning with a lead-off bunt single. The bunt wasn't the big blow, but it portended a shaky first for Jays pitcher R.A. Dickey, who then allowed a two-run homer to Ben Zobrist, before walking Lorenzo Cain, giving up a single to Eric Hosmer and allowing two more runs to score on a passed ball and a sacrifice fly in a mixed bag of misery for Jays fans.

DICKEY DONE EARLY

The 40-year-old knuckleballer has had shaky starts before, but he often settles in and can sometimes turn an outing on its head by throwing five or six scoreless innings after giving up a crooked number in the first. But after Alex Rios homered in the second and Dickey plunked Escobar before walking Cain again, John Gibbons had seen enough. Dickey's start of just 1⅔ innings was his shortest in seven years. "I had trouble arresting the damage," he admitted.

Adapted from Five Moments by Brendan Kennedy first published by the *Toronto Star* on October 21, 2015.

HENDRIKS HEROICS

With the Jays in an early 5-0 hole, Gibbons turned to Liam Hendriks to keep them afloat. The Australian right-hander did just that, throwing 4⅓ scoreless innings while allowing just one base-runner, giving the Jays' offence a chance to climb back in it. For Hendriks it was his longest relief outing in more than two years and the first time he had pitched that many innings in a game since August 27, 2014.

JAYS ON BOARD

Royals starter Chris Young kept the Jays in check for most of the afternoon, but in the third inning Ryan Goins keyed a two-run rally capped by a ground-rule double by Josh Donaldson. It looked then like the Jays might be mounting a bit of a comeback. But Young settled in and retired the next seven batters in a row.

ROYALS ROUT

After Hendriks was expended, Gibbons turned to LaTroy Hawkins to keep the game within reach. When he failed, Ryan Tepera came in. By the time it was over, the Jays trailed by a dozen runs and Gibbons had reluctantly turned to setup man Mark Lowe as well as utility infielder Cliff Pennington, who became the first exclusively position player in baseball history to pitch in a post-season game.

Towel-waving fans at the Rogers Centre rode an emotional roller coaster as the Jays bounced back from several setbacks to push the ALCS to six games.

AL Championship Series
GAME FIVE

TORONTO BLUE JAYS 7 KANSAS CITY ROYALS 1

BRUCE ARTHUR *Toronto Star*
First published October 22, 2015

TORONTO, ONTARIO—It's an exhilarating feeling, flirting with disaster and coming out alive. It must be what tight-rope walkers feel when they reach the other skyscraper or a stuntman feels when the motorcycle lands on the far side of the canyon and doesn't skid out. The Toronto Blue Jays aren't safe yet; they're still on the rope, or in the air. But they're alive and get to keep going.

"We've allowed ourselves the chance to play another game," said Jose Bautista, who took the biggest pitch of Toronto's 7-1 win in game five of the American League Championship Series against the Kansas City Royals and walked away.

The Jays now trail 3-2 in the best-of-seven series, and it looks like it was easy if you only look at the final

First baseman Chris Colabello, a clutch hitter all season, smacks a second-inning homer to put the Blue Jays ahead 1-0. It's a lead they won't surrender.

score. It wasn't, though. It was survival. Disaster has to wait.

It could have gone so wrong, so easily. Marco Estrada was glittering on the mound, a master, and he didn't allow a Kansas City baserunner past second base through six innings. Chris Colabello, this team's closest thing to a baseball vagabond, had homered in the second for a 1-0 lead. But 1-0 against Kansas City is nothing. A 1-0 lead against the Royals is trying to walk the wire with your eyes closed.

In the bottom of the sixth inning, Bautista came to the plate against brilliant Royals starter Edinson Volquez with two on and no outs. He worked the count full, then fouled off rocket after rocket: 97 miles per hour, 97, 97, 98. You felt like Toronto's season was out there, staying alive.

And then Bautista took a curveball at the knees, he half-waved his bat and it was called a ball. Bautista, the Greek God of Telling You What the Strike Zone Is and What It Is Not, starting walking, the way you walk if you're trying to bluff your way past security. "You could argue I got the benefit of a borderline call," Bautista said, which for him is an extraordinary admission. Asked how

"You could argue I got the benefit of a borderline call."

Blue Jays slugger **Jose Bautista**

confident he was taking the pitch, he said, "I wasn't, but I did. So I was relieved."

The Royals protested, manager Ned Yost said he couldn't get an umpire's attention to appeal because the building was so loud and MLB's official website and Fangraphs both made the pitch look like a strike, while Brooks Baseball did not.

Edwin Encarnacion walked too and two batters later Troy Tulowitzki cleared the bases with a double, healing shoulder blade and all. It was 5-0, and some of the weight came off.

Volquez told reporters that his catcher Sal Perez told him home plate umpire Dan Iassogna had apologized for the non-call on Bautista. Perez told Sam Mellinger of the

Kansas City Star that, no, that hadn't happened. Either way, like Ryan Goins letting the ball drop in game two, it opened the door. The Jays smashed through.

And, still, this could have been a disaster. In the seventh, Jays manager John Gibbons got David Price up in the bullpen, two days before he was scheduled to pitch a hypothetical game six.

Estrada had allowed two long fly balls in the fifth and in the sixth he had to carefully navigate a two-out walk. The safety valve was Price, who was smashed in his only relief appearance in the last five years, against Texas. Price doesn't even usually throw two days before he pitches. This would have been crazy.

Outfielder Jose Bautista is safe at first on an infield hit in the fourth inning. He will reach first again in the sixth on a controversial walk and score as Troy Tulowitzki breaks open a tense 2-0 game with a three-run double.

Jays starter Marco Estrada shut down the Kansas City offence, allowing just one run on three hits. His effort not only kept his team's hopes alive—he also set up the rest of the pitching staff for game six and possibly game seven.

But it nearly happened, which tells you a little about Gibbons' willingness to throw dice with routine and rhythm and what he thinks of his own bullpen. Estrada got Eric Hosmer to fly out to left and, in so doing, he saved the Jays from the Royals and he saved them from himself.

"That really worked out perfectly, the fact that we didn't need David tonight so he could throw Friday," said Gibbons. "The way our pitching staff and bullpen was lined up today, it couldn't happen any better."

Gibbons has two relievers he trusts, and maybe three starters, and he is trying to walk this club back from a 3-1 deficit and to the World Series on a very narrow wire indeed.

Still, the Jays played their fourth elimination game in 11 days and they are still playing. Now Price gets another chance at playoff redemption on regular rest in the place where he came undone last week and, if the Jays survive, Marcus Stroman will pitch a game seven, the city on his shoulders.

"It's a lot of pressure and there's not a lot of room for mistakes," said Bautista. "I'd say hopefully, if we get to the World Series, we're going to take that experience to our advantage."

It's a narrow wire but they haven't fallen yet. They aren't looking down, either.

FAST FACTS

The Blue Jays have played four elimination games in 11 days and won them all.

Blue Jays closer Roberto Osuna mops up in the ninth inning to secure a 7-1 victory and then confirms to Jose Bautista that the Royals are done and dusted.

FIVE MOMENTS

ESTRADA'S 1-2-3 FIRST

Royals shortstop Alcides Escobar had led off each of the series' previous four games with a hit, twice giving the Royals an early lead. But Jays starter Marco Estrada retied Escobar on a routine groundout to open game five. "It was huge getting Escobar out on the first pitch of the game," catcher Dioner Navarro said. It was the first of nine straight outs for Estrada, who took a one-hitter into the eighth inning.

COLA-BLAST-O

With Estrada cruising, the Jays were able to score first for just the second time in the series when Chris Colabello cranked a solo home run off Edinson Volquez in the second inning. "We definitely needed that," manager John Gibbons said. "Especially in a game like this, you score first—even though it was not a lot of runs—you can breathe a little easier." It was Colabello's third career homer off Volquez.

BAUTISTA BATTLES

In the sixth inning, with the Jays still holding onto that slim 1-0 lead, Volquez ran into some trouble when he walked Ben Revere to lead off the inning and then plunked Josh Donaldson. Bautista then worked a masterful 10-pitch walk, fouling off five straight pitches. "They keep nibbling around the edges of the plate and they're getting some calls and some they don't," Bautista said.

TULO COMES THROUGH

After Bautista's 10-pitch battle loaded the bases, Volquez walked Edwin Encarnacion to hand the Jays their second run. Royals manager Ned Yost then called upon flame-throwing reliever Kelvin Herrera. He first struck out Chris Colabello but shortstop Troy Tulowitzki swung at Herrera's first pitch—a 99 mph fastball—and drove it into the gap for a game-breaking, bases-clearing double.

PEREZ BREAKS THE GOOSE EGG

It was too little, too late for the Royals but Salvador Perez's homer with two outs in the eighth inning broke Estrada's shutout. It was the only extra-base hit Estrada allowed all game, coming after he became the first Jays pitcher to throw seven consecutive scoreless innings in a playoff game since Jimmy Key in game four of the 1992 World Series. Estrada retired 21 of his first 23 batters before Perez's homer.

Adapted from Five Moments by Brendan Kennedy first published by the *Toronto Star* on October 22, 2015.

AL Championship Series
GAME SIX

TORONTO BLUE JAYS 3 KANSAS CITY ROYALS 4

BRUCE ARTHUR *Toronto Star*
First published October 24, 2015

KANSAS CITY, MISSOURI—After everything—after David Price's early mistakes, after a chin-bearded kid pulled a likely double out of the sea and onto dry land, after Jose Bautista cut the lead in half, after Price calmed down, after Fox flashed a graphic that promoted a Mets–Royals World Series in the seventh inning, after Bautista saved Toronto again with a bad ankle, after the rains came . . .

After that novella of a baseball game the Blue Jays were 90 feet away from a tie and couldn't come all the way back and fell 4-3 in game six of the American League Championship Series. They lost the series, four games to two.

"We got very far but, with this team, we should have won the whole thing," said pitcher Marco Estrada. "It's the way baseball is. The best team doesn't always win.

With the Blue Jays trailing 2-0 in the third inning, Jose Bautista turned on a Yordano Ventura fastball and drove it deep into the left field stands for a solo home run.

That's just the way baseball is. It's a crazy sport. It's not like basketball or football where the best team's probably going to win. You just never know.

"But you tip your hat to the Royals. They battled. They didn't give up, either."

The Royals deserve all kinds of credit. After Toronto had come back to tie the game, and after a 45-minute rain delay, closer Roberto Osuna walked leadoff batter Lorenzo Cain in the bottom of the eighth, and when Eric Hosmer hit the ball to right field Bautista threw to second rather than down the line to keep the run from scoring.

Cain ran smart and hard, and was waved home by third-base coach Mike Jirschele. It was a gutsy call. Several Jays said Bautista made the right decision. 4-3, Royals.

"It was definitely a dangerous play on [Cain's] part," said Jays catcher Russell Martin. "He was lucky [shortstop Troy Tulowitzki] didn't get a clean grip on the baseball."

And in the top of the ninth, against killer closer Wade Davis, Russell Martin got a leadoff single, and Dalton Pompey pinch-ran and stole second and third like it was nothing, and he was 90 feet away, no outs.

Dioner Navarro, pinch-hitting, struck out swinging. Ben Revere, a contact hitter if nothing else, took a called strike two that was well off the plate, and struck out on the next pitch.

"It was terrible. It was terrible," said Revere, who made a wall-scraping catch to keep it close in the bottom of the eighth. "It changed the whole game. If it's a ball it's a 3-1 count and he has to throw me a strike. Instead it's 2-2 and now . . . it's a terrible call. You can't call that. [The strike zone] was good until the Royals got the lead. With the closer they have, he's already tough enough as it is."

Revere, realizing he couldn't risk ejection, destroyed a trash can in the dugout.

It was left to Josh Donaldson, the best player in the American League, or close enough, and Davis. Davis allowed seven earned runs in his first 73 innings pitched this season. Best on best.

Donaldson grounded out to third on a 2-1 count, and it was over. Hell of a game. Hell of a season.

"I feel sad and happy at the same time," said Osuna. "Sad because we lost, and we worked really hard this year, and I'm happy with what we did this year."

"Obviously we don't feel great about the situation now. But give it some time, give it some time to breathe a little bit," said Donaldson. "Coming into spring training next year, I feel like we'll have some momentum. There's been a lot of learning throughout this season for a lot of guys, including myself, and I feel like it can only make you better in the end."

"I thought we played really well," said first baseman Chris Colabello. "I don't think anybody was ready for it to end. Even down 2-0, 3-1, I don't think there was a second where we didn't think we were going to win the game. You know, I know at some point there's only one team left standing, but this is a great group. It's a shame it had to end."

Jays starter David Price surrendered a home run in each of the first two innings and then buckled down to keep the Blue Jays within striking distance.

"This is a great group. It's a shame it had to end."

Jay first baseman **Chris Colabello**

Jays outfielder Ben Revere climbed the left field fence in the seventh inning to make a spectacular catch on a ball hit by Royals catcher Salvador Perez.

The tension had been building all night long. Between the kid with the beard and Fox's Dewey Defeats Truman graphic, it was easy for knee-jerk conspiracies to flourish. But conspiracies, in sports and elsewhere, are often just incompetence in a different jacket.

No, what happened was Price got drilled early and settled down late, giving up just five hits and striking out eight. He allowed a first-inning home run to former teammate Ben Zobrist and he allowed Mike Moustakas to hit a ball just hard enough that it could be pulled over a wall. Price struck out the next two Royals so, theoretically, a double would not have scored. But after a review, the home run did.

It's not fair but that's baseball. The Cubs could have recovered from Steve Bartman. Jeffrey Maier grabbed a Derek Jeter home run but the Yankees won the series in five games anyway.

The Jays had seven innings to score three runs, or more. They stranded two leadoff runners in the fifth on a ball Donaldson hit 114 mph, and balls that travelled between 110–114 mph this year resulted in a .728 batting average. So it goes. Toronto had won four straight elimination games. They needed a fifth.

And in the eighth inning of a 3-1 game, Bautista delivered. He'd already smashed a solo shot in the third, and Yost tried not to bring Davis in the eighth, and he told Fox it was because he'd seen the weather forecast.

And with Ben Revere at first, Bautista smoked a 96 mph fastball from Ryan Madson to left to tie the game. Bautista kept them alive in game five against Texas and gave them life again. The throw was unfortunate. The homers were grand.

"What a performance by Jose," said Martin. "He loves being in that situation. He loves those big situations."

FAST FACTS

Royals relievers allowed just 7 earned runs in the series. Jays relievers allowed 17 earned runs.

"It's the way baseball is. The best team doesn't always win."

Jays pitcher **Marco Estrada**

So this is how it ends. Colabello and Donaldson were talking the other day about the best way to approach baseball and they settled on a maxim of sorts: Care so much that you don't care. It's about focusing in so much that you can let go, that you don't wind yourself into a knot. Donaldson appears to have mastered it this season; Colabello, for his part, says he has never felt as comfortable in his own skin as he has this year.

"In the post-season, there's so much at stake on every pitch, every moment's so huge," Colabello, who took a preposterously long and winding road to the big leagues, said after the Jays won game five. "There's a reason that this team is here and that team's on that side. I think they're the two best teams in the American League.

"There's so much emotion in the games and, when you're a kid you grow up dreaming about playing in the big leagues and things like that, but when you play in atmospheres like this, where the crowds are loud, and people are so in tune with every pitch, it just takes you to another level as an athlete, and I think sometimes you're able to do things that you didn't know you were capable of.

"I know for me, that's what I've lived for my whole life. That's what I've always wanted."

That's what Jays fans have wanted for two decades, and a little more, and it's what they got. Now Price seems likely to walk as a free agent, and general manager Alex Anthopoulos is a question mark for incoming president Mark Shapiro to answer, and soon. The future is far from certain.

But what a year. This team gave you almost everything you could have asked for. They just needed a little more.

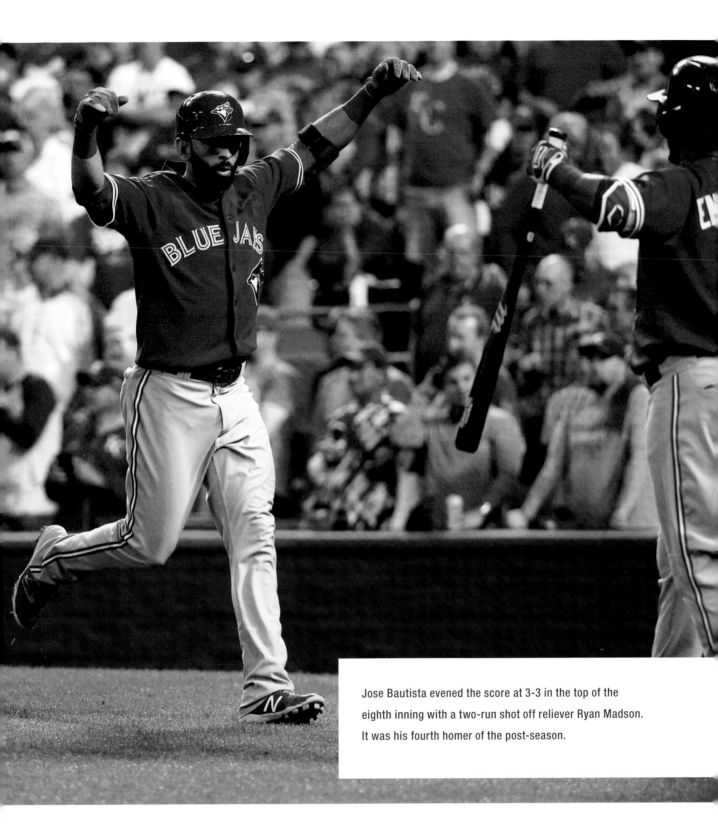

Jose Bautista evened the score at 3-3 in the top of the eighth inning with a two-run shot off reliever Ryan Madson. It was his fourth homer of the post-season.

End of the line—Josh Donaldson heads off the field after grounding out in the top of the ninth inning with two out and two runners on base.

FIVE REASONS THE BLUE JAYS LOST THE ALCS

BLOWING GAME TWO

If you're David Price and the Jays, this is the game you most want back. Price cruised through his first six innings, allowing just a single hit. Then Ben Zobrist led off the seventh with a pop-up into shallow right field. Ryan Goins looked like he had it, but suddenly gave way and the ball landed between him and Jose Bautista. Five batters later everything had unraveled for the Jays. Single, single, RBI groundout, single, double and the Royals led 5-3.

ROYALS HIT, JAYS DIDN'T

The Jays had their chances in the series—more than the Royals, in fact—but they didn't capitalize as often as the Royals. The Jays hit just .204 with runners in scoring position, more than 80 points lower than their league-best mark in the regular season. The Royals, meanwhile, hit .422 with runners at second or third in nine fewer chances. And not only did the Royals outhit the Jays, they also out-homered them seven to five.

K.C. BULLPEN ROCKS

The seeds of this disadvantage were sown in the Jays' division series against Texas when Brett Cecil suffered a torn calf muscle. That left the Jays without arguably their best overall reliever. The Royals also lost closer Greg Holland to Tommy John surgery in September. But even without Holland, Royals relievers allowed just seven earned runs in the series. The Jays bullpen, by contrast, allowed 17 earned runs.

HOME-FIELD ADVANTAGE

Manager John Gibbons decided to rest his starters for two games after they had clinched the division title in Baltimore. The Jays tied for the best home record in the AL this season and were clearly more comfortable at the Rogers Centre than they were at Kauffman Stadium. There's no guarantee that the Jays would have won those two games in Baltimore. But that certainly won't stop the second guessing, particularly since the Jays finished just two games behind the Royals.

DAVID PRICE

The 30-year-old lefty was superb in his first two months as a Blue Jay. He won 9 of 11 starts, including pivotal victories over the New York Yankees. Perhaps the Jays messed with his routine by pitching him out of the bullpen in the division series and warming him up in the league championship. But when it comes down to it, he just didn't pitch well enough in the playoffs when they needed him most.

Adapted from Five Reasons by Brendan Kennedy first published by the *Toronto Star* on October 24, 2015.

The future looks bright

RICHARD GRIFFIN *Toronto Star*
Adapted from a column first published on October 24, 2015

The Blue Jays will not be content with reaching the post-season this October. There seems to be a legitimate window open for at least one more year based on the number of key offensive players who are under contract for next season.

That being said, there are huge question marks on the pitching side that will have to be addressed by the new front office headed by president Mark Shapiro.

In terms of a 2016 batting order, it's amazing the Jays lose a grand total of only 526 plate appearances from players who finished the season with them. The list of players likely to be shown the door includes catcher Dioner Navarro, outfielder Ezequiel Carrera plus infielders Cliff Pennington, Munenori Kawasaki and Darwin Barney. Everyone else is under club control.

That means the opening day lineup could feature Ben Revere, Josh Donaldson, Jose Bautista, Edwin Encarnacion, Troy Tulowitzki, Chris Colabello or Justin Smoak, Russell Martin, Kevin Pillar and Ryan Goins. The bench could be chosen from among Michael Saunders, Devon Travis, Dalton Pompey and Josh Thole.

It's on the pitching side the Jays will need to do a lot of heavy lifting to ensure they have what it takes to repeat as a playoff team.

Eligible for free agency from among the pitchers will be David Price, Mark Buehrle, Marco Estrada, LaTroy Hawkins, Mark Lowe and Jeff Francis. That group of six pitchers cost the Jays a combined $33 million (U.S.) in 2015—if you calculate the amount the Jays had to pay Price after acquiring him at the end of July.

The biggest question mark of all is Price and whether to try to re-sign him or spend those resources elsewhere. If it's the latter, the Jays would have to believe that having Marcus Stroman for a full season at the top of the rotation would be equivalent to bringing back Price—it wouldn't be.

What will Price be looking for? He is 30, so he will want seven years—who wants to negotiate another contract at 35 or 36? He will want between $22 million and $30 million per season, because that is the range of the top nine pitcher salaries in Major League history.

The list includes Clayton Kershaw (seven years/$215M), Max Scherzer (seven/$210M), Justin Verlander (seven/$180M), Felix Hernandez (seven/$175M), C.C. Sabathia (seven/$161M), Masahiro Tanaka (seven/$155M), Jon Lester (six/$155M), Zack Greinke (six/$147M) and Cole Hamels (six/$144M). Price fits nicely within that group.

It says here the Jays will not bring Price back. As for Buehrle, he will either retire or take a short-term contract with a team in the U.S. Midwest. That's 24 wins between the two veterans that will need to be replaced.

As for Estrada, the Jays have an excellent chance of bringing him back for a three- or four-year deal at a reasonable number. He's already 32 and Toronto is where he has had his first real success.

Remember, the Jays are not just trying to compete in 2016, they will be trying to at least repeat their trip to the post-season. They can be looking at a rotation of Stroman, R.A. Dickey, Estrada, Aaron Sanchez and Drew Hutchison.

Sanchez was a starter until he was hurt in June and was rehabbing as a starter before the team realized they needed immediate help in the eighth inning. He will likely be a starter again next spring.

That quintet of potential starters combined for only 665 innings and 48 wins. Clearly, without Price, there will need to be at least one major signing or a trade.

The bullpen will also need help but that's an area easier to restock via free agency, with good scouting and a little bit of luck.

These playoffs showed how thin the Jays' bullpen actually is in terms of arms that manager John Gibbons trusts. The injury to Brett Cecil and the family issue for Aaron Loup that caused him to miss three games highlighted the organization's weakness from the left side.

From the bullpen's right side, 42-year-old Hawkins will retire and Lowe will be difficult to re-sign. Liam Hendriks was impressive for most of the season as a hard-throwing middle man, and Osuna is the likely first choice to repeat in the closer's role. That's pretty thin, given all the promising young arms from the farm system that were dealt away in the last week of July.

There is a lot of off-season work to be done, but the returning position players that led the major leagues in runs scored give the Jays a nice head start.

TORONTO STAR

John D. Cruickshank – Publisher

Edward A. MacLeod – COO Print

Michael Cooke – Editor

Jane Davenport – Managing Editor

Jennifer Quinn – Sports Editor

Taras Slawnych – Visuals Editor

Phil Bingley – Book Project Editor

Ed Cassavoy – Director, Reader Engagement & Content
Commercialization–Print

Robin Graham – Managing Director, Torstar
Syndication Services

Debbie Gaudet – Research

Established 1892 –

Joseph E. Atkinson, Publisher, 1899–1948

Contributors

Bruce Arthur

Rosie DiManno

Richard Griffin

Bob Hepburn

Brendan Kennedy

David Rider

Verity Stevenson

Mark Zwolinski

PHOTO CREDITS